By Devon K
and The Sum It C

ISLA

Summarized

A Concise Guide to Islamic Beliefs, History, Law, and Spirituality – Understanding Islam, the Qur’an, Shariah, Sufism, and Muslim Traditions

West Agora Int

Timisoara 2025

WEST AGORA INT S.R.L.

ISLAM Summarized
Copyright © 2025
West Agora Int

Published by West Agora Int
Edited by West Agora Int
Cover Art by West Agora Int

Unlock the Wisdom of One of the World's Great Religions—Clearly, Powerfully, and Without Bias.

For over 1,400 years, Islam has shaped civilizations, inspired profound spiritual traditions, and influenced the course of world history. Yet, for many, it remains misunderstood—overshadowed by stereotypes and misconceptions.

ISLAM Summarized is your gateway to a clear, compelling, and comprehensive understanding of Islam. Whether you are a seeker of knowledge, a student of world religions, or someone searching for clarity beyond the noise, this book will guide you through the essential pillars of Islamic faith, law, and philosophy.

Who was the Prophet Muhammad, and how did he change the world?

What does the Qur'an truly teach?

How do Shariah, Sufism, and Islamic ethics shape Muslim life?

What are the core theological differences between Sunni and Shi'a Islam?

How has Islam influenced science, art, and global history?

What role does Islam play in today's world—and where is it headed?

This is not just another academic textbook—it is a journey into the heart of Islam, written for those who crave real understanding. Thought-provoking, insightful, and powerfully engaging, ISLAM Summarized distills centuries of tradition into an accessible, well-researched, and deeply rewarding read.

If you want to understand Islam—not through sensationalism, but through knowledge—this book belongs in your hands.

Are you ready to discover the depth and beauty of one of the world's most influential faiths? ***Start reading today!***

TABLE OF CONTENTS

Islamic Jargon

A

Adab – Islamic etiquette, manners, and ethical conduct.

Adhan – The call to prayer, recited by the muezzin five times a day.

Ahl al-Bayt – The "People of the House," referring to the family of Prophet Muhammad.

Ahl al-Kitab – "People of the Book," referring to Jews and Christians in Islamic theology.

Ahadith (sing. Hadith) – Sayings, actions, and approvals of Prophet Muhammad.

Ahl al-Sunnah wa'l-Jama'ah – The mainstream Sunni Muslim community.

Akhlaq – Islamic ethics and moral character.

Al-Fatiha – The opening chapter of the Qur'an, recited in every unit of prayer.

Alhamdulillah – "Praise be to God," an expression of gratitude.

Amanah – Trust, responsibility, or moral duty in Islam.

Amin – Equivalent to "Amen," said at the end of supplications.

Ansar – "Helpers," the residents of Medina who supported Prophet Muhammad.

Aqidah – Islamic theology and creed.

Arkan al-Islam – The five pillars of Islam.

Asr – The third of the five daily prayers, performed in the afternoon.

B

Badr – The first major battle in Islam, fought in 624 CE.

Baitul Maqdis – Another name for Al-Aqsa Mosque in Jerusalem.

Barakah – Divine blessings and spiritual abundance.

Bid'ah – Religious innovation; often viewed negatively.

Bismillah – "In the name of Allah," recited at the beginning of actions.

Burqa – A full-body covering worn by some Muslim women.

C

Caliph (Khalifa) – Successor to the Prophet Muhammad as leader of the Muslim community.

D

Da'wah – The call to Islam, or Islamic missionary work.

Dajjal – The false messiah (Antichrist) in Islamic eschatology.

Dalil – Evidence or proof in Islamic jurisprudence.

Dhimmi – Non-Muslims living under Muslim rule with legal protection.

Dhuhr – The second of the five daily prayers, performed at noon.

Dua – Supplication or personal prayer.

Dunya – The temporal, worldly life.

E

Eid al-Adha – "Festival of Sacrifice," commemorating Prophet Ibrahim's (Abraham's) willingness to sacrifice his son.

Eid al-Fitr – "Festival of Breaking the Fast," marking the end of Ramadan.

F

Fajr – The first of the five daily prayers, performed at dawn.

Fard – Religious obligation; something that is mandatory in Islam.

Fiqh – Islamic jurisprudence and the interpretation of Shariah.

Fitnah – Trial, tribulation, or social discord.

Fitrah – The innate natural disposition of humans towards God.

G

Ghayb – The unseen or hidden reality known only to Allah.

Ghusl – The full-body ritual purification.

H

Hadith – Recorded sayings and actions of Prophet Muhammad.

Hafiz – A person who has memorized the entire Qur'an.

Halal – Permissible according to Islamic law.

Haram – Forbidden according to Islamic law.

Hijab – Modest dress for Muslim women, often referring to the headscarf.

Hijrah – The migration of Prophet Muhammad from Mecca to Medina.

Huda – Guidance, often referring to divine guidance from Allah.

I

Ibadah – Worship and devotion to God.

Iblis – The name of Satan in Islam.

Iftar – The meal to break the fast during Ramadan.

Ijma' – Consensus of Islamic scholars on religious issues.

Ijtihad – Independent reasoning in Islamic jurisprudence.

Imam – A leader of prayer or an Islamic scholar.

Iman – Faith or belief in Islam.

InshaAllah – "If God wills," commonly used in conversation.

Islamophobia – Prejudice or discrimination against Muslims.

Isnad – The chain of narration for Hadith.

J

Jahannam – Hell in Islamic eschatology.

Jahiliyyah – The period of ignorance before Islam.

Janazah – Islamic funeral prayer.

Jannah – Paradise in Islamic eschatology.

Jihad – Struggle or striving in the way of God, both spiritual and military.

Jinn – Spiritual beings created from smokeless fire.

Jizya – A tax paid by non-Muslims under Muslim rule.

Jumu'ah – The Friday congregational prayer.

K

Kaaba – The sacred cubic structure in Mecca, the holiest site in Islam.

Kafir – A disbeliever or one who rejects faith.

Khalifa – Successor or caliph, leader of the Muslim community.

Khutbah – The sermon given during Jumu'ah (Friday) prayer.

L

Laylat al-Qadr – "Night of Power," a special night in Ramadan believed to be the night the Qur'an was revealed.

M

Mahdi – The prophesied guided one who will appear before the Day of Judgment.

Madhhab – A school of Islamic jurisprudence (Hanafi, Maliki, Shafi'i, Hanbali).

Maqasid al-Shariah – The higher objectives of Islamic law.

Masjid – Mosque, the place of Islamic worship.

Mawlid – Celebration of the Prophet Muhammad's birthday.

Mi'raj – The ascension of Prophet Muhammad to heaven.

Mufti – A scholar qualified to issue religious rulings (fatwas).

N

Nafs – The self, soul, or ego in Islamic spirituality.

Nikah – Islamic marriage contract.

Niyyah – Intention, a key component of acts of worship.

P

Polygamy – The practice of a man having multiple wives, permitted with conditions in Islam.

Q

Qadar – Divine predestination in Islam.

Qiblah – The direction of prayer, towards the Kaaba in Mecca.

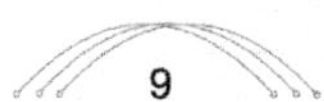

Quran – The holy book of Islam, revealed to Prophet Muhammad.

R

Ramadan – The ninth month of the Islamic calendar, a month of fasting.

Riba – Interest, prohibited in Islamic finance.

Ruqyah – Islamic spiritual healing through Qur'anic recitation.

S

Sadaqah – Voluntary charity.

Sahabah – The companions of Prophet Muhammad.

Salah – The five daily prayers in Islam.

Sawm – Fasting in Islam, especially during Ramadan.

Shariah – Islamic law.

Shirk – Associating partners with Allah; considered the gravest sin in Islam.

Sunnah – The way of the Prophet Muhammad.

T-Z

Tafsir – Interpretation of the Qur'an.

Tawhid – The concept of monotheism in Islam.

Ulama – Islamic scholars.

Ummah – The global Muslim community.

Wudu – Ritual ablution before prayer.

Zakat – Obligatory charity in Islam.

Introduction to Islam

Definition, origins, significance, and global presence.

Defining Islam

Islam is a monotheistic religion that emerged in the 7th century CE in the Arabian Peninsula. The term "Islam" itself is derived from the Arabic root s-l-m, which means "peace" or "submission." In its religious context, Islam signifies submission to the will of Allah (God). A follower of Islam is called a Muslim, meaning "one who submits."

Islam is built upon the fundamental belief in the absolute oneness of God (Tawhid), a concept that forms the cornerstone of the religion. It acknowledges a direct and personal relationship between the individual and Allah, without intermediaries. Islam is more than just a religion; it is a comprehensive way of life (deen), encompassing spiritual, moral, social, legal, and political dimensions.

The faith is encapsulated in the Shahada, or declaration of faith, which states: "La ilaha illa Allah, Muhammadur Rasul Allah" ("There is no god but Allah, and Muhammad is His Messenger"). This simple yet profound statement unites Muslims across different cultures and traditions.

Origins of Islam

The roots of Islam trace back to Prophet Muhammad (570–632 CE), who is regarded by Muslims as the final prophet in a long line of messengers that includes Adam, Noah, Abraham, Moses, and Jesus. The religion formally began in the early 7th century CE in Mecca, Arabia (modern-day Saudi Arabia), when Muhammad received divine revelations from Allah through the Angel Jibreel (Gabriel).

These revelations were gradually compiled into the Qur'an, which Muslims believe to be the literal word of God. Unlike previous scriptures, such as the Torah and the Gospels, the Qur'an is considered by Muslims to be unaltered and eternal, preserved in its original form since its revelation.

Muhammad's early message emphasized monotheism, social justice, and moral rectitude, which led to resistance from the ruling tribes of Mecca, who saw Islam as a threat to their polytheistic traditions. In 622 CE, Muhammad and his followers migrated to Medina in an event known as the Hijra (Migration). This event marks the beginning of the Islamic calendar and led to the establishment of an Islamic state. Over the next decade, Islam spread rapidly throughout the Arabian Peninsula, culminating in the conquest of Mecca in 630 CE and the unification of the region under Islamic rule.

Following Muhammad's death in 632 CE, Islam continued to expand through conquests, trade, and missionary efforts, spreading across the Middle East, North Africa, Persia, and beyond.

The Significance of Islam

Islam is not just a religious belief system but a holistic framework that guides all aspects of a Muslim's life. Its significance is multi-dimensional:

Theological Significance: Islam affirms a direct and personal relationship with Allah. It provides clarity on human existence, divine purpose, and the afterlife.

Moral and Ethical System: The religion outlines a comprehensive ethical code, emphasizing justice (adl), compassion (rahma), and accountability (tawba).

Legal and Social System: The Shariah (Islamic law) governs personal conduct, family life, business transactions, and societal justice.

Cultural and Civilizational Influence: Islamic teachings have shaped art, architecture, philosophy, science, and governance for over a millennium.

Community and Unity: The Ummah (global Muslim community)

embodies a sense of belonging, transcending race, nationality, and culture.

Islam's Global Presence

Islam is the second-largest religion in the world, with over 1.9 billion adherents, constituting approximately 25% of the global population. It is the fastest-growing major religion, driven by high birth rates and increasing conversions.

Geographical Distribution

Islam is present in nearly every country, but its largest populations are concentrated in specific regions:

South Asia: Home to over 600 million Muslims, with Indonesia (231 million) being the largest Muslim-majority country, followed by Pakistan, India, and Bangladesh.

Middle East and North Africa (MENA): The religious and historical heartland of Islam, including countries such as Saudi Arabia, Egypt, Iran, and Turkey.

Sub-Saharan Africa: Countries like Nigeria, Sudan, and Somalia have significant Muslim populations.

Europe: Islam is the second-largest religion, with large communities in France, Germany, and the UK, mostly due to migration.

North America: The U.S. and Canada have growing Muslim communities, with Islam being the fastest-growing religion in both countries.

Diversity Within Islam

Despite the unity of belief, Islam is diverse in its interpretations and practices. Some key distinctions include:

Sunni Islam: The majority branch (85-90%), following the traditions of the Prophet (Sunnah).

Shi'a Islam: A significant minority (10-15%), emphasizing the leadership of the Prophet's family.

Sufism: A mystical branch focusing on spiritual purification and direct experience of God.

Other Movements: Ahmadiyya, Ibadiyya, and modern reformist movements also exist.

These distinctions have shaped theological discourse, political history, and cultural expressions within Islam.

Islam's Contribution to World Civilization

Throughout history, Islam has played a pivotal role in advancing science, philosophy, medicine, and the arts. During the Islamic Golden Age (8th–14th centuries), Muslim scholars in cities like Baghdad, Cordoba, and Cairo made groundbreaking contributions in astronomy, mathematics, medicine, and philosophy. Some notable scholars include:

Al-Khwarizmi (Mathematics): Developed algebra (Al-Jabr).

Ibn Sina (Medicine): Wrote The Canon of Medicine, a standard medical text for centuries.

Al-Farabi and Ibn Rushd (Philosophy): Integrated Greek philosophy with Islamic thought.

Al-Biruni (Astronomy and Geography): Measured the Earth's radius with remarkable accuracy.

Islamic architecture, with its distinctive domes, minarets, and intricate geometric designs, remains one of the most celebrated forms of artistic expression.

Conclusion

Islam is a comprehensive faith that encompasses theological, legal, ethical, and social dimensions. With its emphasis on monotheism, divine guidance, and community, it has shaped civilizations and continues to influence global affairs. Understanding Islam requires not only an appreciation of its core beliefs and practices but also a recognition of its rich history, cultural diversity, and ongoing evolution.

As Islam continues to grow, its presence in global

discourse—whether through interfaith dialogue, academic study, or societal contributions—remains indispensable. This book will explore Islam in its entirety, providing a well-rounded foundation for anyone seeking knowledge about one of the world's most significant religious traditions.

The Life of Prophet Muhammad

His biography, mission, and impact on world history

A Child of the Desert: The Birth and Early Years of Muhammad

In the arid lands of 6th-century Arabia, amidst a world of tribal rivalries, commerce, and idolatry, a child was born in the city of Mecca who would one day change the course of human history. Muhammad ibn Abdullah, later known as the Prophet of Islam, was born in the year 570 CE, a time referred to by historians as the Year of the Elephant. His birth occurred into the powerful Quraysh tribe, a dominant clan that controlled the sacred Kaaba and the lucrative trade routes passing through Mecca.

Yet, despite his noble lineage, Muhammad's early life was marked by profound hardship. His father, Abdullah, died before Muhammad was born, leaving his mother, Aminah, to raise him alone. However, tragedy struck again when, at the tender age of six, Muhammad lost his mother, leaving him an orphan. He was then placed under the care of his grandfather, Abdul Muttalib, a revered elder of the Quraysh. But within two years, death claimed Abdul Muttalib as well, leaving young Muhammad in the hands of his paternal uncle, Abu Talib.

Under Abu Talib's guardianship, Muhammad grew up in a world where survival depended on loyalty, honor, and strength. He worked as a shepherd in his youth, tending to the flocks of Mecca's people, a role that instilled in him patience, humility, and a deep connection to nature. Later, he became a merchant, earning a reputation for his honesty and integrity, earning him the title Al-Amin (the Trustworthy) among the people of Mecca.

The Marriage to Khadijah and a Life of Reflection

As Muhammad's reputation as a fair and skilled trader spread, he caught the attention of a wealthy and noble widow, Khadijah bint Khuwaylid, a successful merchant in her own right. She proposed marriage to Muhammad, despite being fifteen years his senior. Their union was one of mutual love and respect, and for many years, Muhammad lived a life of relative peace. They were blessed with several children, including Fatimah, who would later play a significant role in Islamic history.

Yet, even as a successful merchant and devoted husband, Muhammad found himself deeply troubled by the state of Meccan society. Corruption, idolatry, and social injustices were rampant, and the worship of multiple deities dominated the city. Seeking solace, he would retreat to the Cave of Hira, a secluded spot in the mountains outside Mecca, where he would meditate and contemplate the mysteries of existence.

The Revelation and the Birth of Islam

It was in the stillness of the Cave of Hira that everything changed. In the year 610 CE, at the age of 40, Muhammad experienced a moment that would forever alter human history. As he sat in quiet reflection, he was suddenly enveloped by an overwhelming presence—the Angel Jibreel (Gabriel), who commanded him to "Recite!" (Iqra). Bewildered and frightened, Muhammad responded that he was unable to recite, but the angel repeated the command:

"Recite in the name of your Lord who created—
Created man from a clinging substance.

Recite! And your Lord is the Most Generous—

Who taught by the pen—

Taught man that which he knew not." (Qur'an 96:1-5)

These words, the first verses of the Qur'an, signified the beginning of Muhammad's prophetic mission. Overwhelmed, he rushed home to Khadijah, who comforted him and assured him that he was not forsaken. She became his first believer, marking the start of what would soon become a revolution of faith.

The Struggles and Persecution in Mecca

Muhammad's message was simple yet radical: There is only one God, Allah, and He alone deserves worship. This struck at the very core of Meccan society, which thrived on the economic benefits of polytheism, as the Kaaba housed numerous idols worshiped by various tribes. When Muhammad began preaching publicly, he faced mockery, scorn, and ultimately, violent persecution.

The Quraysh elites, led by figures like Abu Lahab and Abu Jahl, sought to silence him. They ridiculed his claims of prophecy, accused him of madness, and even resorted to torturing his followers. Slaves who embraced Islam, such as Bilal ibn Rabah, were subjected to brutal whippings and left to die under the scorching desert sun. Yet, despite the suffering, the faith of these early Muslims remained unshaken.

One of Muhammad's greatest personal losses during this time was the death of Khadijah in 619 CE, followed closely by the passing of Abu Talib, his protective uncle. With his greatest supporters gone, Muhammad's position in Mecca became increasingly perilous.

The Hijra: A New Beginning in Medina

Faced with mounting threats, Muhammad and his followers sought refuge in the oasis town of Yathrib (later called Medina). In 622 CE, Muhammad made the perilous journey from Mecca to Medina in what became known as the Hijra (Migration). This event was so pivotal that it marked the beginning of the Islamic calendar.

In Medina, Muhammad was not merely a prophet—he became a statesman and leader, establishing the first Islamic state. He drafted the Constitution of Medina, a groundbreaking document that ensured rights and religious freedom for Muslims, Jews, and pagans alike. The community flourished, and Islam grew in strength.

The Conquest of Mecca and the Final Sermon

After years of conflict, including battles such as Badr, Uhud, and the Trench, the balance of power shifted. In 630 CE, Muhammad and his followers triumphantly entered Mecca, reclaiming the city peacefully. The idols within the Kaaba were destroyed, and the sanctuary was rededicated to the worship of Allah alone.

Two years later, during his Farewell Pilgrimage, Muhammad delivered his final sermon, a speech that laid the foundation for Islamic ethics and human rights. He proclaimed:

"O people, your Lord is One, and your father is one. You are all from Adam, and Adam was created from dust. The most honored among you in the sight of Allah is the most righteous."

Shortly after, in 632 CE, at the age of 63, Muhammad passed away in Medina, leaving behind a legacy that would transform the world.

The Impact of Muhammad on World History

Muhammad's influence extended far beyond Arabia. Within a century of his passing, Islam had spread across the Middle East, North Africa, and parts of Europe and Asia. His teachings inspired advancements in science, philosophy, and governance, shaping civilizations for centuries.

Today, over 1.9 billion people revere him as the last Prophet and follow his teachings, making him one of the most influential figures in history. His life serves as a testament to resilience, justice, and unwavering faith.

In understanding Muhammad's journey—from orphan to merchant, from prophet to leader—we grasp not only the story of a man but the unfolding of a divine mission that continues to guide millions.

The Qur'an: Islam's Holy Book

Origins, structure, themes, and methods of interpretation (Tafsir).

Origins, Structure, Themes, and Methods of Interpretation (Tafsir)

For over fourteen centuries, the Qur'an has stood as the foundational text of Islam, guiding the lives, spirituality, and intellectual traditions of nearly two billion Muslims worldwide. It is not merely a book of scripture but is regarded by believers as the literal word of God (Allah), revealed to Prophet Muhammad as a divine message to humanity. To truly understand Islam, one must first understand its sacred text—how it was revealed, structured, and interpreted.

The Origins of the Qur'an

The Qur'an's origins are intimately tied to the life and mission of Prophet Muhammad. In the year 610 CE, while meditating in the Cave of Hira outside Mecca, Muhammad received his first revelation from Angel Jibreel (Gabriel). The angel commanded him to "Recite!" (Iqra), marking the beginning of a 23-year-long period of divine revelation.

Unlike other religious scriptures, which were often written down long after their inception, the Qur'an was revealed to Muhammad gradually over two decades—addressing specific events, answering questions, and providing guidance to the nascent Muslim community. The revelations, sometimes lengthy and sometimes just a few verses, came in different circumstances: in times of peace and conflict, strength and hardship, personal reflection and communal challenges.

As Muhammad was unlettered and did not write, his companions memorized the verses and wrote them down on materials like parchment, palm leaves, and bones. The preservation of the Qur'an was meticulous, and by the time of Muhammad's passing in 632 CE, the entire revelation was memorized by many of his followers. It was later compiled into a single book under the leadership of Caliph Abu Bakr, ensuring its preservation for future generations.

The Structure of the Qur'an

The Qur'an consists of 114 chapters (Surahs), which vary in length, with some being only a few verses and others spanning multiple pages. The longest chapter, Surah Al-Baqara, contains 286 verses (Ayahs), while the shortest, Surah Al-Kawthar, consists of only three verses.

Although it is not arranged chronologically in the order it was revealed, the Qur'an follows a divine organization. The chapters are generally structured from longer to shorter, with exceptions in thematic coherence. The Qur'an is divided into 30 equal sections (Juz') to facilitate reading over a month, particularly during the month of Ramadan, when Muslims aim to complete its recitation.

The Qur'an is written in classical Arabic, and its linguistic beauty is often considered unmatched. It employs a rhythmic, poetic style, with rhetorical devices, metaphors, and repetitions that enhance both its recitation and memorization. Its powerful prose has been a source of deep inspiration for poets, scholars, and thinkers throughout Islamic history.

Major Themes of the Qur'an

The Qur'an is more than just a set of legal or religious ordinances—it is a comprehensive guide that speaks on faith, morality, law, history, and human destiny. Several key themes dominate its verses:

Tawhid (The Oneness of God)

The concept of absolute monotheism is the heart of the Qur'an's message. The most fundamental principle of Islam is that there is no deity but Allah, and He has no partners or equals. Surah Al-Ikhlas (Chapter 112) encapsulates this belief in just a few words:

"Say, He is Allah, the One. Allah, the Eternal Refuge. He neither begets nor is born, nor is there to Him any equivalent."

Prophethood and Revelation

The Qur'an asserts that Muhammad is the last in a long line of prophets, who include Adam, Noah, Abraham, Moses, and Jesus. It acknowledges previous scriptures like the Torah, Psalms, and Gospels, affirming their divine origins while emphasizing that the Qur'an is the final and most complete revelation.

The Afterlife and Human Accountability

One of the most frequently recurring themes in the Qur'an is the Hereafter (Akhirah)—the reality of heaven (Jannah) and hell (Jahannam). The Qur'an reminds humanity that life is a test and that individuals will be judged based on their faith and deeds. Verses paint vivid descriptions of both paradise and punishment, urging people to live righteously.

Moral and Social Justice

The Qur'an provides detailed guidance on ethics and justice, emphasizing honesty, kindness, charity, and patience. It condemns social ills such as oppression, corruption, and arrogance, while advocating for the protection of the poor, orphans, and vulnerable groups. It instructs believers to conduct themselves with integrity in business, family life, and governance.

Laws and Guidance for Life

While the Qur'an is primarily a spiritual guide, it also contains legal injunctions concerning marriage, trade, inheritance, crime, and warfare. It lays the foundation for Shariah (Islamic law), though its interpretation requires supplementary sources like the Hadith (Prophetic traditions).

The Science of Qur'anic Interpretation (Tafsir)

Understanding the Qur'an requires more than just reading its verses—context is essential. This is where Tafsir (exegesis or interpretation) plays a crucial role. Tafsir seeks to explain the meanings, reasons for revelation (Asbab al-Nuzul), and application of Qur'anic teachings.

Some of the most famous classical Tafsir scholars include:

Ibn Kathir (1300-1373 CE) – His Tafsir al-Qur'an al-Azim remains one of the most widely referenced works.

Al-Tabari (839-923 CE) – His Tafsir al-Tabari is one of the earliest and most comprehensive commentaries.

Al-Qurtubi (1214-1273 CE) – His work focuses on legal rulings derived from the Qur'an.

Modern scholars continue to explore Tafsir in light of contemporary issues, ensuring that the Qur'an remains a living document that speaks to each generation.

The Qur'an's Influence on Islamic Civilization

The impact of the Qur'an extends far beyond the religious sphere. It has influenced art, literature, philosophy, and governance in Muslim societies for centuries. The science of Arabic grammar was developed largely to preserve the purity of Qur'anic recitation. Calligraphy and architectural designs of mosques and manuscripts often incorporate Qur'anic verses. The Qur'an has also inspired movements for social reform, urging leaders and scholars to address injustices in their societies.

Even today, the Qur'an remains the most widely memorized book in the world, with millions committing its entire text to memory. Its recitation is considered an act of worship, and its teachings continue to shape the ethical and spiritual lives of Muslims worldwide.

Conclusion

The Qur'an is more than just Islam's sacred scripture; it is the heartbeat of the faith, a divine revelation that continues to illuminate, inspire, and challenge those who engage with its message. Whether as a source of spiritual solace, moral guidance, or legal framework, the Qur'an stands as a timeless testament to divine wisdom, offering a blueprint for a just and meaningful life. To understand Islam is to understand the Qur'an—a book that remains at the center of Muslim devotion and scholarship to this day.

Hadith and Sunnah: The Prophetic Tradition

Definition, classification, key collections, and their role in Islamic law and practice.

Islam is a faith rooted in divine revelation, but understanding its teachings requires more than just the Qur'an. Alongside the Qur'an, there exists another indispensable source of guidance: the Hadith and Sunnah of Prophet Muhammad. Together, they form the Prophetic Tradition, which provides crucial insight into how Islamic principles should be applied in everyday life.

While the Qur'an is the literal word of Allah, the Hadith consists of the sayings, actions, and approvals of Prophet Muhammad, while the Sunnah refers to his way of life. Muslims regard the Prophet as the perfect example of how to live according to God's will, and thus, the Hadith and Sunnah serve as a practical demonstration of Islamic teachings.

This chapter will explore the definitions of Hadith and Sunnah, their classification, the major collections, and their role in Islamic law and practice.

Definition of Hadith and Sunnah

What is Hadith?

The term Hadith (plural: Ahadith) means "narration" or "report" in Arabic. It refers to recorded statements, actions, and silent approvals of Prophet Muhammad. Each Hadith consists of two parts:

Isnad (Chain of Transmission): The list of narrators who passed down the Hadith, tracing it back to the Prophet.

Matn (Text of the Hadith): The actual content of the narration, which could be a statement, an action, or an approval.

The Hadith serves as a supplementary source to the Qur'an,

offering context, explanation, and elaboration on Islamic teachings. Without Hadith, many Qur'anic commandments would remain abstract. For example, the Qur'an commands Muslims to perform prayer (Salah) but does not provide details on how to do so—those details come from Hadith.

What is Sunnah?

The Sunnah refers to the lifestyle, habits, and practices of Prophet Muhammad. While Hadith is the documented record of the Prophet's words and actions, Sunnah represents the actual way he lived his life.

The Sunnah is categorized into three types:

Sunnah Qawliyyah (Verbal Teachings): Statements made by the Prophet (e.g., supplications, ethical guidelines).

Sunnah Filiyyah (Actions of the Prophet): How he performed daily tasks, such as prayer, fasting, and charity.

Sunnah Taqririyyah (Silent Approvals): Incidents where the Prophet witnessed an act and did not object, implying his approval.

Both Hadith and Sunnah are integral to Islam because they demonstrate how to live according to the Qur'anic message.

Classification of Hadith

The science of Hadith classification developed as a rigorous discipline to ensure the authenticity of narrations. Islamic scholars analyzed Hadith based on the reliability of the chain of transmission (Isnad) and the integrity of the text (Matn).

Hadith are classified into different categories:

Based on Authenticity

Sahih (Authentic): A Hadith with a strong and unbroken chain of narrators known for their reliability and precision. Example: Sahih al-Bukhari and Sahih Muslim contain only Sahih Hadith.

Hasan (Good): A Hadith with a trustworthy chain but slightly weaker than Sahih.

Da'if (Weak): A Hadith with a broken or unreliable chain of

narrators. Such Hadith are not used for legal rulings.

Mawdu' (Fabricated): A Hadith that was falsely attributed to the Prophet. Scholars reject these as inauthentic.

Based on the Number of Narrators

Mutawatir (Mass Transmitted): A Hadith narrated by so many people across different generations that it is impossible for it to have been fabricated.

Ahad (Solitary Narration): A Hadith narrated by a few individuals, making it less certain than Mutawatir Hadith.

These classifications ensure that only reliable and verifiable reports are used in Islamic law and teachings.

Major Hadith Collections

Over centuries, scholars compiled Hadith collections, meticulously verifying each narration to preserve authentic traditions. The most respected collections are known as the Six Canonical Books (Kutub al-Sittah):

Sahih al-Bukhari (d. 870 CE) – Compiled by Imam al-Bukhari, it is the most authentic Hadith collection, containing over 7,000 Hadith.

Sahih Muslim (d. 875 CE) – Compiled by Imam Muslim, known for its rigorous authenticity criteria.

Sunan Abu Dawood (d. 889 CE) – Focuses on legal Hadith related to Islamic jurisprudence (Fiqh).

Jami' al-Tirmidhi (d. 892 CE) – Includes Hadith with commentary on their authenticity.

Sunan an-Nasa'i (d. 915 CE) – Contains detailed Hadith related to worship and social conduct.

Sunan Ibn Majah (d. 887 CE) – The last of the Six Books, containing both strong and weak Hadith.

Other important Hadith collections include Muwatta Malik and Musnad Ahmad, which also preserve valuable traditions.

The Role of Hadith and Sunnah in Islamic Law and Practice

Hadith and Sunnah are essential sources of Islamic law (Shariah), second only to the Qur'an. They clarify Qur'anic injunctions, provide moral and ethical guidance, and establish legal rulings.

1. Interpretation of the Qur'an

Many Qur'anic verses require explanation. For example, the Qur'an commands:

"Establish prayer and give Zakat" (2:110)

But it does not explain how to pray or how much Zakat to give—this knowledge comes from Hadith.

2. Development of Islamic Jurisprudence (Fiqh)

Islamic scholars used Hadith to develop four major schools of Fiqh (Hanafi, Maliki, Shafi'i, and Hanbali). These schools rely on Hadith to derive legal rulings for marriage, trade, crime, and worship.

3. Ethical and Social Guidance

Hadith provide ethical teachings on honesty, kindness, and patience. A famous Hadith states:

"The best among you are those who have the best character." (Sahih al-Bukhari)

4. Daily Life and Worship

Muslims model their lives after the Prophet's Sunnah, from how they eat and sleep to how they interact with others.

Conclusion

Hadith and Sunnah form the living tradition of Islam, providing practical guidance where the Qur'an offers general principles. The meticulous classification and preservation of Hadith ensure that Muslims today follow teachings that remain authentic and reliable. Whether shaping Islamic law or guiding everyday conduct, Hadith and Sunnah remain indispensable pillars of the faith—a legacy that continues to illuminate the path of believers worldwide.

The Articles of Faith (Iman)

Belief in God, angels, scriptures, prophets, the Day of Judgment, and divine decree.

Faith (Iman) is the spiritual foundation of Islam, the internal conviction that shapes a Muslim's relationship with Allah and the world. While Islam is often recognized for its outward acts of worship, such as prayer and fasting, these practices stem from an inner belief system that governs a Muslim's worldview. At the core of this belief system are the Six Articles of Faith, which every Muslim must accept as part of their creed.

The Articles of Faith define how a believer perceives the divine, the unseen, human purpose, and ultimate destiny. They encompass belief in God (Allah), angels, scriptures, prophets, the Day of Judgment, and divine decree (Qadar). Together, these tenets offer a comprehensive framework for understanding existence, morality, and the afterlife.

1. Belief in Allah (Tawhid: The Oneness of God)

The cornerstone of Islamic faith is Tawhid, the absolute oneness of Allah. Islam asserts that there is only one God, who is eternal, self-sufficient, and beyond human comprehension. This is encapsulated in the fundamental declaration of faith (Shahada):

"There is no god but Allah, and Muhammad is His messenger."

Allah's names and attributes are described in the Qur'an, with 99 divine names (Asma' al-Husna) that illustrate His qualities, such as:

Ar-Rahman (The Most Merciful)

Al-'Aleem (The All-Knowing)

Al-Qadir (The All-Powerful)

Islam strongly emphasizes monotheism, rejecting any concept of God having partners, offspring, or limitations. This belief sets it apart from polytheistic traditions and even the Trinitarian concept of Christianity, which Islam views as a departure from pure monotheism.

To believe in Allah means to:

Recognize His sovereignty over creation.

Worship Him alone without associating partners (shirk).

Trust in His wisdom and guidance, even in times of hardship.

The Qur'an states:

"Say, He is Allah, the One. Allah, the Eternal Refuge. He neither begets nor is born, nor is there to Him any equivalent." (Surah Al-Ikhlas, 112:1-4)

This belief shapes every aspect of a Muslim's life, from worship to ethical conduct, as Allah is the ultimate judge and the source of all moral guidance.

2. Belief in Angels (Mala'ika)

In Islam, angels are unseen spiritual beings created by Allah from light (nur). Unlike humans, they do not possess free will; they exist solely to obey Allah's commands and carry out divine tasks.

The most well-known angels in Islamic tradition include:

Jibreel (Gabriel): The angel of revelation who delivered the Qur'an to Prophet Muhammad.

Mikail (Michael): Responsible for providing sustenance and rainfall.

Israfil: The angel who will blow the trumpet to signal the Day of Judgment.

Azrael: The angel of death (Malak al-Mawt), who takes souls at the appointed time.

Kiraman Katibin: Two angels assigned to each person, recording their deeds—one for good and one for bad.

Munkar and Nakir: Angels who test the soul in the grave after death.

Belief in angels reinforces the idea that Allah's will and knowledge extend beyond human perception. These divine beings serve as intermediaries between Allah and creation, ensuring that the cosmic order functions perfectly.

3. Belief in Divine Scriptures (Kutub Allah)

Islam teaches that Allah has revealed divine scriptures to various prophets throughout history to guide humanity. The Qur'an, as the final and unaltered word of God, confirms the existence of earlier revelations:

The Torah (Tawrat) – Given to Prophet Moses (Musa).

The Psalms (Zabur) – Given to Prophet David (Dawud).

The Gospel (Injil) – Given to Prophet Jesus (Isa).

The Scrolls (Suhuf) – Given to Prophet Abraham (Ibrahim).

Muslims believe that while the original scriptures were divinely revealed, they have been altered or lost over time, whereas the Qur'an remains unaltered and preserved. The Qur'an itself states:

"Indeed, it is We who sent down the Qur'an, and indeed, We will be its guardian." (Surah Al-Hijr, 15:9)

Thus, while Muslims respect earlier scriptures, they believe that the Qur'an supersedes previous revelations and contains the most complete and final guidance.

4. Belief in Prophets (Nubuwwah)

Islam recognizes a long chain of prophets, sent by Allah to guide humanity. These include well-known figures such as Adam, Noah, Abraham, Moses, Jesus, and Muhammad.

The final prophet, Muhammad, is regarded as the Seal of the Prophets (Khatam an-Nabiyyin), meaning that no further prophets will come after him. His mission was universal, extending to all of humanity, unlike previous prophets who were sent to specific nations.

The role of prophets was to:

Call people to monotheism (Tawhid).

Provide moral and legal guidance.

Warn of consequences for disbelief and injustice.

Prophets are considered sinless in their mission and chosen by Allah, but they remain human beings, not divine.

5. Belief in the Day of Judgment (Yawm al-Qiyamah)

Islam teaches that life on Earth is a test and that all people will be resurrected and judged by Allah on the Day of Judgment.

On this day:

All souls will be brought back to life.

Their deeds will be weighed on a divine scale.

People will be rewarded with Paradise (Jannah) or punished in Hell (Jahannam).

The Qur'an vividly describes the events of the Last Day, including the destruction of the universe, the raising of the dead, and the final judgment.

"Every soul shall taste death. And you will only be given your [full] compensation on the Day of Judgment." (Surah Aal-E-Imran, 3:185)

This belief instills a sense of moral accountability—knowing that every action has consequences in the hereafter.

6. Belief in Divine Decree (Qadar)

The final pillar of faith is belief in Allah's divine decree, also known as Qadar. This means that everything happens according to Allah's knowledge and will, yet human beings are granted free will to make moral choices.

Islam teaches a balance between divine destiny and human responsibility. While Allah's knowledge encompasses all things, people are still responsible for their actions.

"No disaster strikes upon the Earth or among yourselves except that it is in a register before We bring it into being—indeed that, for Allah, is easy." (Surah Al-Hadid, 57:22)

This belief provides comfort in adversity, as Muslims trust that

Allah's plan is just and wise.

Conclusion

The Six Articles of Faith form the foundation of Islamic belief, shaping how Muslims perceive existence, their responsibilities, and their ultimate destiny. These beliefs provide a moral compass, guiding Muslims in their worship, interactions, and worldview. To believe in Islam is to accept these principles wholeheartedly, recognizing that faith is not just an internal conviction but a way of life that manifests in actions, ethics, and devotion to Allah.

The Five Pillars of Islam

A comprehensive study of Shahada (faith), Salah (prayer), Zakat (charity), Sawm (fasting), and Hajj (pilgrimage).

Islam is a religion that is not just about belief but also about practice. It is a way of life, deeply embedded in the daily actions of its followers. At the heart of Islamic practice are the Five Pillars of Islam, which form the foundation of a Muslim's faith and devotion to Allah. These five essential acts of worship—Shahada (Faith), Salah (Prayer), Zakat (Charity), Sawm (Fasting), and Hajj (Pilgrimage)—serve as both a spiritual framework and a practical code of conduct. They guide Muslims in their relationship with God, their communities, and themselves.

For over 1,400 years, these pillars have remained unchanged, binding together Muslims across continents and cultures. Whether a believer is in the bustling streets of Cairo, the quiet villages of Indonesia, or the heart of New York City, the Five Pillars unite all Muslims in a shared expression of faith, discipline, and moral responsibility.

Shahada: The Declaration of Faith

The Shahada is the first and most fundamental pillar of Islam. It is the declaration of faith, a simple yet profound statement that distinguishes a Muslim from a non-Muslim:

"La ilaha illa Allah, Muhammadur Rasul Allah."

"There is no god but Allah, and Muhammad is His Messenger."

This phrase is the essence of Tawhid (the oneness of God), affirming that Allah is the only deity worthy of worship. The second part of the Shahada acknowledges Muhammad as the final prophet, through whom Allah's message was completed.

The Shahada is more than just words; it is a commitment, a

testimony that shapes a Muslim's entire existence. It is whispered into the ears of newborns, recited in daily prayers, and spoken as a final declaration at the moment of death. By sincerely pronouncing the Shahada, one enters the fold of Islam and pledges to live according to its teachings.

The power of the Shahada lies in its simplicity. Unlike other religious traditions that require elaborate rituals for conversion, Islam requires only this sincere testimony. It signifies complete submission to Allah and acceptance of Muhammad's guidance.

Salah: The Daily Prayers

Prayer (Salah) is the second pillar of Islam and the most frequent daily act of worship. It is performed five times a day at prescribed times:

Fajr (before dawn)

Dhuhr (midday)

Asr (afternoon)

Maghrib (just after sunset)

Isha (night)

The Qur'an commands Muslims to establish prayer as an act of devotion:

"And establish prayer and give zakat and bow with those who bow [in worship]." (Surah Al-Baqarah, 2:43)

Each prayer consists of a series of movements and recitations, including standing, bowing, and prostrating—physical expressions of humility before Allah. Before performing Salah, Muslims must perform wudu (ablution), purifying themselves spiritually and physically.

Salah is more than a ritual; it is a direct connection between the believer and Allah. Regardless of status or wealth, every Muslim stands before their Creator in the same way, reinforcing equality and unity. The discipline of Salah also instills punctuality, mindfulness, and spiritual focus, helping Muslims stay connected to their faith throughout the day.

The Friday congregational prayer (Jumu'ah) holds special significance, bringing communities together in mosques for a sermon (khutbah) and communal worship.

Zakat: The Duty of Charity

Islam is not just about individual faith—it is about social responsibility. The third pillar, Zakat, is a form of mandatory charity that ensures economic fairness and helps those in need. Muslims who meet a minimum wealth threshold (Nisab) must give 2.5% of their savings annually to the less fortunate.

The Qur'an commands this act of charity:

"Take, [O Muhammad], from their wealth a charity by which you purify them and cause them increase." (Surah At-Tawbah, 9:103)

Zakat serves multiple purposes:

Purification: It cleanses one's wealth from greed and selfishness.

Social Equity: It reduces poverty by redistributing wealth.

Compassion: It fosters empathy for those who struggle.

The beneficiaries of Zakat include:

The poor and needy

Debtors

Those striving in the path of Allah

Travelers in need

Beyond Zakat, Muslims are encouraged to give Sadaqah (voluntary charity) as an act of generosity.

Sawm: The Fast of Ramadan

Every year, during the Islamic month of Ramadan, Muslims around the world engage in Sawm (fasting), the fourth pillar of Islam. From dawn until sunset, they abstain from food, drink, and other physical needs, focusing instead on spiritual purification and self-discipline.

The Qur'an states:

"O you who have believed, decreed upon you is fasting as it was decreed upon those before you that you may become righteous." (Surah Al-Baqarah, 2:183)

Fasting in Ramadan is not merely about physical deprivation—it is a time of deep spiritual reflection, increased prayer, and charitable giving. It fosters empathy for the poor and instills self-control over desires.

Each day's fast is broken at sunset with the Iftar meal, traditionally beginning with dates and water, following the practice of Prophet Muhammad. The month concludes with Eid al-Fitr, a celebration marked by communal prayers and acts of charity.

Certain individuals, such as the sick, elderly, and travelers, are exempt but must make up for missed fasts or feed the needy.

Hajj: The Pilgrimage to Mecca

The Hajj pilgrimage is the final pillar of Islam and a journey of immense spiritual significance. Every Muslim who is physically and financially able must perform Hajj at least once in their lifetime.

Hajj takes place during the Islamic month of Dhul-Hijjah, drawing millions of pilgrims to Mecca, where they engage in rituals that trace back to Prophet Ibrahim (Abraham). These rituals include:

Tawaf: Circling the Kaaba seven times.

Sa'i: Walking between the hills of Safa and Marwah.

Standing at Arafat: Seeking Allah's forgiveness on the most critical day of Hajj.

Stoning the Devil: Throwing pebbles at symbolic pillars in Mina.

Hajj symbolizes unity, humility, and devotion. Regardless of nationality or social status, all pilgrims wear simple white garments (Ihram) to demonstrate equality before Allah.

The completion of Hajj is celebrated with Eid al-Adha, marked by the sacrifice of an animal, commemorating Ibrahim's willingness to sacrifice his son for Allah's command.

Conclusion

The Five Pillars of Islam are more than religious duties—they are a blueprint for a righteous life. They cultivate faith, discipline, charity, self-control, and unity, guiding Muslims toward spiritual fulfillment and moral responsibility.

By practicing these pillars, Muslims maintain a deep connection with Allah, a sense of community with fellow believers, and a continuous reminder of their purpose in this world and the hereafter. The Five Pillars stand as a testament to Islam's balanced approach to faith, blending worship with ethical conduct and personal development.

Shariah: Islamic Law

Sources, principles, and schools of jurisprudence (Fiqh).

Islam is not just a system of beliefs; it is a comprehensive way of life that governs both spiritual and worldly affairs. At the heart of this system is Shariah, the Islamic legal framework that provides guidance on how a Muslim should live in accordance with divine will. The term Shariah comes from the Arabic root sh-r-ʻ, meaning "the path to be followed"—a metaphor for the way of life that leads to righteousness and justice.

For over 1,400 years, Shariah has played a central role in shaping Islamic civilization, influencing everything from personal conduct and family matters to governance, economics, and criminal law. It is not merely a set of legal rulings but a moral and ethical system, designed to foster social harmony, justice, and adherence to God's commands.

Understanding Shariah requires exploring its sources, principles, and the diverse schools of Islamic jurisprudence (Fiqh) that interpret and apply it.

1. The Sources of Shariah

Shariah is derived from four primary sources, each serving a unique function in Islamic legal reasoning:

1.1 The Qur'an: The Primary Source

The Qur'an is the ultimate and foundational source of Islamic law. It contains numerous legal injunctions, addressing issues such as:

Worship and rituals (prayer, fasting, pilgrimage).

Family law (marriage, divorce, inheritance).

Economic principles (trade, interest, contracts).

Criminal justice (theft, murder, adultery).

While the Qur'an provides the broad framework of law, it does not offer detailed legal codes for every aspect of life. Instead, it lays down general principles that must be interpreted and applied in various contexts.

One of the key legal maxims in the Qur'an states:

"Indeed, Allah commands justice, good conduct, and giving to relatives and forbids immorality, bad conduct, and oppression." (Surah An-Nahl, 16:90)

This verse reflects the overarching goal of Shariah: to establish justice and prevent harm.

1.2 The Sunnah: The Prophetic Tradition

The Sunnah, which includes the Hadith (recorded sayings and actions of Prophet Muhammad), serves as the second source of Shariah. Since the Qur'an often provides general commands, the Sunnah offers practical demonstrations of how these should be implemented.

For example, the Qur'an commands Muslims to pray (Salah), but it does not specify the number of prayers, their timings, or their method. These details are derived from the Sunnah, which records how the Prophet performed them.

1.3 Ijma (Consensus of Scholars)

Since the Qur'an and Sunnah do not explicitly address every possible legal scenario, Islamic jurists developed the principle of Ijma (consensus). If the companions of the Prophet or later scholars unanimously agreed on a ruling, it became a binding precedent.

Ijma was particularly important in the early centuries of Islam, when scholars sought to codify legal principles for emerging social and political issues.

1.4 Qiyas (Analogical Reasoning)

When a new issue arises that is not directly addressed in the Qur'an or Sunnah, scholars use Qiyas (analogy) to derive rulings. This method involves comparing a new case to an existing law based on a shared legal cause ('illah).

For example, the Qur'an forbids alcohol because it intoxicates and leads to harm. Based on Qiyas, scholars extended this prohibition to narcotic drugs, which have a similar effect.

Together, these four sources form the backbone of Shariah, ensuring that Islamic law remains adaptable to changing times while staying true to divine principles.

2. Principles of Shariah

Shariah is guided by five overarching objectives, known as Maqasid al-Shariah (The Goals of Islamic Law). These objectives aim to protect essential human rights and maintain a just society.

2.1 The Five Objectives (Maqasid al-Shariah)

Preservation of Religion (Hifz ad-Din) – Ensuring freedom of worship and protecting Islamic teachings.

Preservation of Life (Hifz an-Nafs) – Safeguarding human life and ensuring personal security.

Preservation of Intellect (Hifz al-Aql) – Promoting education and prohibiting substances that impair the mind.

Preservation of Lineage (Hifz an-Nasl) – Protecting family structures and ensuring the legitimacy of offspring.

Preservation of Wealth (Hifz al-Mal) – Regulating economic transactions and prohibiting fraud and exploitation.

These principles emphasize that Islamic law is not rigid or oppressive but is designed to achieve justice, well-being, and social harmony.

3. Schools of Islamic Jurisprudence (Fiqh)

Over time, differences in interpretation and application of Shariah led to the development of various schools of thought, known as Fiqh (Islamic jurisprudence). While Shariah represents divine law, Fiqh is its human interpretation, which can vary based on context and reasoning.

The four major Sunni schools and their distinctive approaches are:

3.1 The Hanafi School

Founded by: Imam Abu Hanifa (d. 767 CE)

Characteristics: The most flexible school, emphasizing rational reasoning (Istihsan) and local customs (Urf).

Followed in: Turkey, India, Pakistan, and Central Asia.

3.2 The Maliki School

Founded by: Imam Malik ibn Anas (d. 795 CE)

Characteristics: Strongly relies on the practice of the people of Medina as a source of law.

Followed in: North and West Africa.

3.3 The Shafi'i School

Founded by: Imam Al-Shafi'i (d. 820 CE)

Characteristics: A balanced approach, giving equal importance to Qur'an, Sunnah, Ijma, and Qiyas.

Followed in: Egypt, Indonesia, Malaysia, East Africa.

3.4 The Hanbali School

Founded by: Imam Ahmad ibn Hanbal (d. 855 CE)

Characteristics: The most conservative, relying heavily on Hadith and rejecting excessive reasoning.

Followed in: Saudi Arabia, parts of the Gulf region.

The Shi'a legal system, known as Ja'fari Fiqh, follows the teachings of Imam Ja'far al-Sadiq and is predominantly practiced in Iran and parts of Iraq and Lebanon.

Conclusion

Shariah is more than just a legal code; it is a comprehensive system of ethical and legal principles that guide Muslims in every aspect of life. Rooted in the Qur'an, Sunnah, and scholarly reasoning, it ensures justice, morality, and social welfare.

Despite differences in interpretation and schools of Fiqh, the ultimate purpose of Shariah remains the same: to create a just, ethical, and God-conscious society. It continues to be a dynamic and evolving system, adapting to new challenges while remaining true to its divine foundations.

Islamic Theology (Aqidah)

Core beliefs, major theological schools (Ash'ari, Maturidi, Salafi, Mu'tazila).

Islam is not only a religion of practice but also a religion of belief and conviction. At its core lies Aqidah, or Islamic theology, which defines the fundamental doctrines of faith that every Muslim must accept. While the outward expressions of Islam—such as prayer, fasting, and charity—form the framework of a Muslim's life, it is Aqidah that provides the intellectual and spiritual foundation upon which this framework stands.

Islamic theology is built on the principle that faith is not blind acceptance but a reasoned belief in absolute truths. The Qur'an constantly urges believers to reflect, ponder, and use reason to understand the nature of God, existence, and the ultimate purpose of life. Over the centuries, this deep engagement with theological questions has led to the development of various theological schools, each offering a different perspective on how to interpret divine revelation, free will, and the nature of God's attributes.

In this chapter, we explore the core beliefs of Aqidah, followed by an examination of the four major theological schools: Ash'ari, Maturidi, Salafi, and Mu'tazila.

Core Beliefs of Islamic Theology (Aqidah)

The foundation of Aqidah is derived from the Qur'an and the teachings of Prophet Muhammad. While different theological schools have debated various details, the following beliefs are universally accepted across all sects of Islam.

1. Tawhid: The Absolute Oneness of God

At the heart of Islamic theology is Tawhid, the belief in the absolute oneness of Allah. This concept is so fundamental that it is encapsulated in the Shahada (declaration of faith):

"There is no god but Allah, and Muhammad is His Messenger."

Tawhid is not just a rejection of polytheism but also an assertion that God is without partners, equals, or limitations. The Qur'an describes Him as:

"Say: He is Allah, the One. Allah, the Eternal Refuge. He neither begets nor is born, nor is there to Him any equivalent." (Surah Al-Ikhlas, 112:1-4)

This belief in divine unity shapes the Muslim worldview, ensuring that worship is directed only to Allah and that no created being shares in His divinity.

2. Prophethood (Nubuwwah) and the Finality of Muhammad

Muslims believe that Allah has guided humanity through a series of prophets, from Adam to Noah, Abraham, Moses, and Jesus, culminating in Muhammad, the final messenger. These prophets were chosen by God to deliver divine revelation and serve as moral exemplars.

The finality of Muhammad's prophethood (Khatm an-Nabuwwah) is a central tenet of Islamic theology. The Qur'an affirms:

"Muhammad is not the father of any of your men, but he is the Messenger of Allah and the seal of the prophets." (Surah Al-Ahzab, 33:40)

3. Divine Scriptures (Kutub Allah)

Muslims believe in four major scriptures revealed by Allah:

The Tawrat (Torah) given to Moses

The Zabur (Psalms) given to David

The Injil (Gospel) given to Jesus

The Qur'an, revealed to Muhammad as the final and unaltered

word of God

While previous scriptures were distorted or lost, the Qur'an remains unchanged, serving as the final source of divine guidance.

4. The Afterlife (Akhirah) and the Day of Judgment

Islamic theology teaches that this world is temporary and that a final judgment awaits all souls. On the Day of Judgment (Yawm al-Qiyamah), every person will be held accountable for their deeds.

The Qur'an vividly describes the realities of Paradise (Jannah) for the righteous and Hellfire (Jahannam) for the wicked. Belief in the Akhirah instills a sense of moral responsibility, reminding Muslims that their actions in this life determine their fate in the hereafter.

The Major Theological Schools of Islam

Throughout history, Muslims have engaged in deep theological discussions, leading to the development of distinct schools of thought. While they all agree on the core beliefs mentioned above, they differ on issues such as the nature of divine attributes, free will, and reason versus revelation.

1. The Ash'ari School

Founder: Abu al-Hasan al-Ash'ari (d. 936 CE)

Regions: Predominantly followed in North Africa, the Levant, and parts of the Indian subcontinent.

The Ash'ari school emerged as a middle path between strict rationalism and literalism. It sought to balance reason with revelation, arguing that while human intellect is important, it is ultimately limited in understanding divine matters.

God's Attributes: Ash'aris believe that Allah's attributes (e.g., His hands, His face) are real but beyond human comprehension. They accept them without literal interpretation.

Free Will: They take a moderate determinist approach, believing that while humans have limited free will, their actions are ultimately created by Allah.

Ash'arism became the dominant theological school in Sunni Islam, influencing major scholars like Al-Ghazali and Fakhr al-Din al-Razi.

2. The Maturidi School

Founder: Abu Mansur al-Maturidi (d. 944 CE)

Regions: Predominantly followed in Turkey, Central Asia, and the Indian subcontinent.

The Maturidi school is similar to Ash'arism but places a greater emphasis on human reason.

God's Attributes: They believe that Allah's attributes are real and eternal, but humans cannot fully comprehend them.

Free Will: Maturidis argue that humans have more free will than Ash'aris claim. They believe that Allah knows all actions in advance but does not force them.

Maturidism became the official theology of the Ottoman Empire, shaping the beliefs of many Muslims.

3. The Salafi School

Regions: Predominantly followed in Saudi Arabia and parts of the Gulf region.

The Salafi movement rejects theological speculation, advocating for a strictly literal interpretation of Islamic texts.

God's Attributes: They take the literal meaning of Qur'anic descriptions of Allah.

Free Will: Salafis emphasize strict divine control over human actions.

Salafism traces its intellectual roots to Ahmad ibn Hanbal and later reformers like Ibn Taymiyyah and Muhammad ibn Abd al-Wahhab.

4. The Mu'tazila School

Founder: Wasil ibn Ata (d. 748 CE)

Regions: Historically influential in early Islamic history but later declined.

The Mu'tazila school is known for its rationalist approach,

emphasizing human reason over strict textualism.

God's Attributes: They reject the idea that God has attributes distinct from His essence.

Free Will: They strongly advocate for human free will, arguing that Allah does not create human actions.

Despite their intellectual contributions, Mu'tazilism declined due to opposition from mainstream Sunni scholars.

Conclusion

Islamic theology is rich and diverse, reflecting the intellectual depth of Muslim scholars over the centuries. Whether through the Ash'ari and Maturidi balance of reason and revelation, the Salafi emphasis on literalism, or the Mu'tazili rationalist approach, the study of Aqidah continues to shape the spiritual and intellectual life of Muslims. At its core, however, all schools remain united in their devotion to Allah, the Qur'an, and the teachings of Prophet Muhammad.

Islamic Ethics (Akhlaq)

Moral teachings and the pursuit of virtue.

Islam is not merely a religion of rituals and legal codes; it is also a comprehensive system of ethics and morality, shaping the character of individuals and the moral fabric of society. At the heart of Islamic teachings lies Akhlaq, a term derived from the Arabic root kh-l-q, meaning character or disposition. It refers to the moral virtues, manners, and ethical conduct that Islam seeks to instill in its followers.

Akhlaq in Islam is not just about personal refinement but about cultivating a harmonious and just society. It extends to truthfulness, patience, kindness, humility, and justice, influencing interactions between individuals, families, and communities. Prophet Muhammad himself stated:

"I have been sent to perfect noble character." (Musnad Ahmad 8952)

This statement underscores the centrality of ethics in Islam. It is not an optional pursuit but an essential aspect of faith, intertwined with worship and spirituality.

The Foundation of Islamic Ethics

The ethical framework in Islam is rooted in three fundamental sources:

The Qur'an – The primary divine text, containing numerous moral injunctions and ethical principles.

The Sunnah (Prophetic Teachings) – The life and character of Prophet Muhammad serve as a living example of how ethical values should be practiced.

The Concept of Taqwa (God-Consciousness) – Islamic ethics are driven by an awareness that Allah is always watching, reinforcing personal integrity and accountability.

In contrast to secular morality, which often evolves based on societal changes, Islamic ethics are absolute and grounded in divine revelation. However, Islam also recognizes the role of human reasoning (aql) in applying these ethical principles to different times and contexts.

Key Ethical Values in Islam

1. Truthfulness (Sidq) and Honesty (Amanah)

Islam strongly emphasizes truthfulness, considering it a hallmark of faith. The Qur'an states:

"O you who believe! Fear Allah and be with those who are truthful." (Surah At-Tawbah, 9:119)

Lying (kidhb) is condemned in Islam, and hypocrisy (nifaq)—which includes deceit—is regarded as one of the gravest moral failings. The Prophet warned that among the signs of a hypocrite is that:

"When he speaks, he lies. When he makes a promise, he breaks it. And when he is entrusted with something, he betrays the trust." (Sahih al-Bukhari 33)

Thus, truthfulness and honesty are not just personal virtues but foundations of a just and functional society.

2. Patience (Sabr) and Perseverance

One of the most praised virtues in the Qur'an is Sabr (patience), which is essential in facing life's challenges, enduring hardships, and restraining from negative behaviors.

The Qur'an declares:

"Indeed, Allah is with those who are patient." (Surah Al-Baqarah, 2:153)

Patience is particularly emphasized in three areas:

In worship – Remaining consistent in prayer and devotion.

In adversity – Facing trials without despair.

Against sin – Resisting temptations and wrongful desires.

The Prophet once stated:

"The real patience is at the first stroke of a calamity." (Sahih al-Bukhari 1302)

This highlights that patience is not passive resignation but an active virtue that strengthens character.

3. Kindness (Ihsan) and Compassion (Rahmah)

Islamic ethics encourage kindness not only to fellow humans but also to animals and the environment. The Qur'an calls Allah "Ar-Rahman" (The Most Merciful) and commands believers to adopt mercy in their dealings.

Prophet Muhammad was known for his immense kindness, and he stated:

"Allah is kind and loves kindness in all matters." (Sahih Muslim 2593)

Even towards those who wronged him, the Prophet responded with forgiveness and mercy. An example of this is when he pardoned the people of Mecca after its conquest, despite their past hostilities against him.

4. Humility (Tawadhu) and Avoidance of Arrogance

Islam warns against pride and arrogance (kibr), considering them diseases of the heart. The Qur'an warns:

"Do not walk upon the Earth exultantly. Indeed, you will never tear the Earth [apart], and you will never reach the mountains in height." (Surah Al-Isra, 17:37)

True nobility in Islam is not measured by wealth, lineage, or status but by piety and good character. The Prophet emphasized this by stating:

"No one who has an atom's weight of arrogance in his heart will enter Paradise." (Sahih Muslim 91)

Humility allows individuals to treat others with respect, acknowledge their faults, and seek self-improvement.

5. Justice (Adl) and Fairness

Justice (Adl) is one of the fundamental pillars of Islamic morality. The Qur'an repeatedly commands fairness in all aspects of life:

"Indeed, Allah commands justice and good conduct and giving to relatives and forbids immorality and bad conduct and oppression." (Surah An-Nahl, 16:90)

Islamic justice is not limited to legal matters but extends to social, economic, and personal dealings. It requires that:

The rights of the weak are protected.

People are judged without bias or discrimination.

Justice is upheld even against oneself.

The Prophet exemplified this when he stated:

"The most beloved of people to Allah is the one who brings the most benefit to others." (Al-Mu'jam al-Awsat 6192)

6. Generosity (Karam) and Charity (Sadaqah)

Islam teaches that wealth is a trust from Allah, and a Muslim must share it with those in need. Generosity is not only a financial obligation (Zakat) but also an ethical virtue.

The Prophet emphasized this by saying:

"The best of people are those who are most beneficial to others." (Musnad Ahmad 23404)

Generosity extends beyond money—it includes offering time, support, and kind words.

The Prophet Muhammad: The Model of Ethical Excellence

Islamic ethics are best exemplified in the life of Prophet Muhammad. The Qur'an describes him as:

"And indeed, you are of a great moral character." (Surah Al-Qalam, 68:4)

He was known for his truthfulness, patience, humility, kindness, and fairness—all the virtues that define Islamic ethics. His life serves as the ultimate model for moral excellence.

A famous example of his patience and mercy was when an old woman who used to throw trash on him fell ill. Instead of retaliating, he visited her and expressed concern, which led her to accept Islam.

Conclusion

Islamic ethics (Akhlaq) is not a set of abstract ideals but a practical guide for daily life. It shapes individual behavior, family relations, and societal harmony. Unlike legal obligations, which focus on external actions, Akhlaq focuses on internal character development, ensuring that good deeds arise from a pure heart and sincere intention.

By embodying truthfulness, patience, kindness, humility, justice, and generosity, a Muslim not only fulfills religious duties but also contributes to a moral and just society. Ultimately, the pursuit of virtue in Islam is a journey of self-purification, leading to closeness with Allah and eternal success in the hereafter.

Islamic Mysticism: Sufism

Origins, practices, major Sufi orders, and key figures.

Islam, as a religion, encompasses not just the legal and theological dimensions of human existence but also the spiritual and mystical aspects of faith. At the heart of this mystical dimension lies Sufism, a spiritual tradition that seeks to cultivate a deep, personal connection with Allah through love, devotion, and inner purification. While the outward aspects of Islam—such as prayer, fasting, and charity—are essential, Sufism emphasizes the inner transformation that leads to closeness with the Divine.

Sufism, known in Arabic as Tasawwuf, is not a sect or a distinct branch of Islam but rather a spiritual methodology that exists within both Sunni and Shi'a traditions. It is a path that aspires toward Ihsan (spiritual excellence), as described by Prophet Muhammad when he said:

"Ihsan is to worship Allah as if you see Him, and if you do not see Him, know that He sees you." (Sahih Muslim 8:1)

This pursuit of Ihsan defines the Sufi way of life, emphasizing love, knowledge, and the purification of the soul. Over centuries, Sufism has produced great scholars, poets, and mystics, leaving a profound impact on Islamic civilization.

Origins of Sufism

The origins of Sufism can be traced back to the time of Prophet Muhammad, whose life exemplified the principles of spiritual devotion, asceticism, and divine love. His companions, particularly figures such as Abu Bakr, Ali, and Salman al-Farsi, embodied these mystical qualities and passed them on to future generations.

The term Sufi is believed to derive from "suf," meaning wool, referring to the simple woolen garments worn by early ascetics. Another interpretation connects it to "safa," meaning purity, signifying the quest for a purified heart.

As Islamic civilization expanded, Sufism began to develop into a distinct spiritual discipline. By the 8th and 9th centuries, influential figures such as Hasan al-Basri (d. 728) and Rabia al-Adawiyya (d. 801) laid the foundations for Sufi thought, emphasizing detachment from worldly desires and the love of Allah above all else.

By the 12th century, Sufism had formalized into organized brotherhoods (Tariqas), each with its own unique practices, teachings, and lineage of spiritual masters (Shaykhs). These Sufi orders played a crucial role in spreading Islam, particularly in Persia, India, Africa, and the Ottoman world.

Core Practices of Sufism

Sufism is centered around spiritual purification, divine love, and the remembrance of Allah. The following are some of the core practices that define the Sufi path:

1. Dhikr (Remembrance of God)

One of the most important practices in Sufism is Dhikr, the constant remembrance of Allah's names and attributes. This is performed individually or in groups, often accompanied by rhythmic breathing, chanting, or movement.

The Qur'an states:

"Verily, in the remembrance of Allah do hearts find rest." (Surah Ar-Ra'd, 13:28)

Different Sufi orders emphasize different forms of Dhikr, some reciting La ilaha illa Allah (There is no god but Allah), while others focus on the 99 names of Allah.

2. Muraqaba (Meditation and Contemplation)

Sufis engage in deep meditation, contemplating the presence of Allah in their lives. This practice, known as Muraqaba, involves focusing one's heart on the Divine, seeking spiritual insight and enlightenment.

This method resembles the mystical experiences of early Muslim saints, such as Al-Hallaj and Bayazid Bistami, who spoke of their overwhelming experience of divine love.

3. Sama (Spiritual Music and Poetry)

Sama, meaning "listening", is the practice of using music, poetry, and dance to heighten spiritual awareness. The most famous example is the whirling dance of the Mevlevi (Whirling Dervishes), founded by Jalal al-Din Rumi in Turkey.

Sama is seen as a means of transcending the ego and drawing closer to Allah, often accompanied by the poetry of Rumi, Hafiz, and Ibn Arabi.

4. The Sufi Master and Spiritual Lineage

A central aspect of Sufism is the relationship between the disciple (Murid) and the spiritual master (Shaykh or Pir). The Shaykh serves as a guide, leading the disciple along the spiritual path through teachings, discipline, and personal mentorship.

Sufi orders trace their spiritual lineage (Silsila) back to Prophet Muhammad, establishing a chain of transmission that validates their teachings.

Major Sufi Orders (Tariqas)

Sufism developed into several Tariqas (spiritual orders), each with unique approaches to divine realization. Some of the most influential include:

1. The Qadiriyya Order

Founded by: Shaykh Abdul Qadir al-Jilani (d. 1166, Baghdad)

Characteristics: One of the oldest Sufi orders, emphasizing charity, humility, and service to others.

Influence: Spread across the Middle East, North Africa, and South Asia.

2. The Naqshbandiyya Order

Founded by: Bahauddin Naqshband (d. 1389, Central Asia)

Characteristics: Emphasizes silent Dhikr (remembrance) and strict adherence to the Sunnah.

Influence: Prominent in Turkey, India, and the Balkans.

3. The Chishtiyya Order

Founded by: Khwaja Moinuddin Chishti (d. 1236, India)

Characteristics: Focuses on love, tolerance, and music (Sama).

Influence: Played a key role in spreading Islam in South Asia.

4. The Mevlevi Order

Founded by: Jalal al-Din Rumi (d. 1273, Turkey)

Characteristics: Known for whirling dance and poetry, emphasizing divine love.

Influence: Still active in Turkey, with followers worldwide.

5. The Tijaniyya Order

Founded by: Ahmad al-Tijani (d. 1815, North Africa)

Characteristics: Stresses intense Dhikr and social reform.

Influence: Prominent in West Africa and parts of the Arab world.

Key Sufi Figures in History

Sufism has produced some of the most profound spiritual thinkers and poets in history. Among them:

Jalal al-Din Rumi (d. 1273) – Author of Masnavi, one of the greatest mystical poetry collections.

Ibn Arabi (d. 1240) – Developed the philosophy of "Unity of Being" (Wahdat al-Wujud).

Rabia al-Adawiyya (d. 801) – One of the earliest Sufi women, known for her doctrine of divine love.

Al-Hallaj (d. 922) – Martyred for his bold mystical statements, such as "I am the Truth".

Conclusion

Sufism remains one of the most enduring and transformative aspects of Islamic spirituality. It is a path that seeks love, knowledge, and purification, offering a deeply personal relationship with Allah. Despite historical opposition from legalistic scholars, Sufism has continued to thrive, influencing art, poetry, and philosophy worldwide.

Through its emphasis on divine love, inner purification, and service to humanity, Sufism continues to inspire millions of Muslims, guiding them toward a deeper understanding of faith and existence.

Islamic Philosophy

Influential thinkers (Al-Farabi, Avicenna, Al-Ghazali, Ibn Rushd) and key ideas.

Islamic civilization has long been a center of intellectual and philosophical inquiry. From the earliest centuries of Islam, scholars sought to understand the nature of existence, the relationship between reason and revelation, and the ultimate purpose of human life. These pursuits gave rise to Islamic philosophy, a tradition deeply rooted in Greek, Persian, and Indian intellectual heritage while remaining fundamentally connected to Islamic theological and mystical thought.

Islamic philosophy, or Falsafa, emerged as an attempt to harmonize reason and faith, balancing the revealed truths of the Qur'an with rational inquiry. While some scholars viewed philosophy as an essential tool for understanding the world and strengthening faith, others saw it as a potential danger to Islamic doctrine. This dynamic tension led to one of the most profound intellectual debates in Islamic history, producing some of the greatest minds in medieval thought.

In this chapter, we explore the key figures of Islamic philosophy—Al-Farabi, Avicenna, Al-Ghazali, and Ibn Rushd—and the lasting influence of their ideas.

The Rise of Islamic Philosophy

Islamic philosophy flourished between the 9th and 12th centuries, a period when Muslim scholars translated and preserved Greek philosophical texts, particularly the works of Plato and Aristotle. The House of Wisdom (Bayt al-Hikma) in Baghdad played a crucial role in this intellectual movement, where Muslim thinkers engaged with Greek thought, integrating it with Islamic theology and metaphysics.

While early Islamic philosophy was influenced by Neoplatonism and Aristotelian logic, it developed its own unique framework, addressing questions such as:

What is the nature of the soul?

Can reason lead to knowledge of God?

How do divine revelation and rational thought coexist?

What is the purpose of human existence?

These questions shaped the discourse of Islamic metaphysics, ethics, epistemology, and political philosophy, leading to the emergence of distinct philosophical schools.

Al-Farabi (872–950 CE): The Second Teacher

Abu Nasr Al-Farabi, known as "the Second Teacher" (after Aristotle), was one of the earliest and most influential Muslim philosophers. Born in Central Asia, he mastered a wide range of subjects, including logic, metaphysics, music, and political theory.

Key Ideas:

The Theory of Emanation:

Al-Farabi adopted Neoplatonic cosmology, proposing that the universe emanates from a single, divine source (Allah) in a hierarchical order. He described a chain of intellects, leading from God to the material world, with human intellect playing a crucial role in understanding divine wisdom.

Political Philosophy and the Ideal State:

Al-Farabi's most famous work, The Virtuous City (Al-Madina al-Fadila), was inspired by Plato's Republic. He argued that the ideal ruler should be a philosopher-king, combining wisdom, morality, and political acumen—a concept that influenced later Islamic and European political thought.

Harmonizing Religion and Philosophy:

Al-Farabi believed that reason and revelation do not contradict each other but rather complement one another. He held that prophets and philosophers seek the same truths—prophets express them symbolically, while philosophers use rational discourse.

Through his work, Al-Farabi laid the foundation for Islamic metaphysics and political thought, earning him the title of the first great Muslim philosopher.

Avicenna (Ibn Sina, 980–1037 CE): The Master of Medicine and Metaphysics

Perhaps the most famous Muslim philosopher, Avicenna (Ibn Sina), was a towering intellect of the Islamic Golden Age. Born in Persia, he became a polymath, excelling in medicine, philosophy, astronomy, and logic. His most influential works include The Book of Healing and The Canon of Medicine, the latter of which remained a standard medical textbook in Europe for centuries.

Key Ideas:

The Concept of Necessary Existence:

Avicenna argued that God is the "Necessary Being" (Wajib al-Wujud), meaning that His existence is self-evident and does not depend on anything else. This idea became a cornerstone of Islamic metaphysics.

The Soul and Immortality:

He proposed a dualistic view of the soul, asserting that human souls are independent of the body and survive after death. This belief influenced later discussions on the afterlife and divine justice.

The Relationship Between Faith and Reason:

Avicenna believed that philosophy and religion are not contradictory, but he also held that rational inquiry can reach truths that revelation conveys in a symbolic form.

Avicenna's ideas shaped both Islamic and Western philosophy, and his influence extended into Scholastic thought, particularly among figures like Thomas Aquinas.

Al-Ghazali (1058–1111 CE): The Critic of Philosophers

While Al-Farabi and Avicenna sought to harmonize philosophy with Islam, Al-Ghazali took a different approach. A theologian, mystic, and philosopher, Al-Ghazali became one of the most influential critics of rationalist philosophy, arguing that pure reason alone is insufficient to grasp divine truth.

Key Ideas:

The Incoherence of the Philosophers (Tahafut al-Falasifa):

In this landmark work, Al-Ghazali refuted Avicenna and other philosophers, particularly their ideas on eternal causality and the nature of God's knowledge. He argued that philosophy could not explain divine mysteries, and he emphasized the importance of revelation and spirituality.

The Role of Sufism:

After experiencing a personal crisis, Al-Ghazali turned to Sufism, advocating that true knowledge of God comes through spiritual experience, not just rational speculation. His work The Revival of the Religious Sciences became a cornerstone of Islamic spirituality.

The Limits of Human Reason:

He contended that while reason is valuable, it cannot fully comprehend divine will. Faith and personal experience, he argued, were more reliable pathways to understanding Allah.

Al-Ghazali's critique led to the decline of philosophy in the Islamic world and the rise of more mystical and theological approaches to Islam.

Ibn Rushd (Averroes, 1126–1198 CE): The Defender of Reason

In response to Al-Ghazali, Ibn Rushd (Averroes) emerged as the great defender of philosophy. A scholar from Andalusia (Muslim Spain), he sought to revive rationalist thought, emphasizing the compatibility of Islam and Aristotelian philosophy.

Key Ideas:

The Incoherence of the Incoherence:

In this famous work, Ibn Rushd refuted Al-Ghazali's arguments, asserting that philosophy and reason are essential tools for understanding faith.

Double Truth Theory:

He proposed that there are two kinds of truth—one based on reason and the other on faith—and that both can coexist without conflict.

Influence on European Thought:

While his ideas were largely rejected in the Islamic world, they became highly influential in medieval Europe, inspiring figures like Thomas Aquinas and Dante.

Conclusion

Islamic philosophy represents one of the most profound intellectual traditions in world history. From Al-Farabi's political philosophy to Avicenna's metaphysics, from Al-Ghazali's theological critiques to Ibn Rushd's defense of reason, these scholars shaped not only Islamic thought but also Western intellectual traditions.

Their debates continue to resonate today, as Muslims and non-Muslims alike seek to understand the relationship between faith, reason, and the search for ultimate truth.

Islam and Science

Contributions of Muslim scholars in mathematics, medicine, astronomy, and philosophy.

Throughout history, civilizations have risen and fallen on the strength of their intellectual pursuits. The Islamic Golden Age, spanning roughly from the 8th to the 14th century, was one of the most remarkable periods of scientific advancement in world history. During this time, Muslim scholars, drawing upon the knowledge of ancient civilizations, made groundbreaking contributions to mathematics, medicine, astronomy, and philosophy—advancements that would later shape the Renaissance and the modern scientific world.

This flourishing of knowledge was deeply rooted in Islam's emphasis on learning. The Qur'an itself encourages intellectual pursuit, with verses such as:

"Read! In the name of your Lord who created." (Surah Al-Alaq, 96:1)

Prophet Muhammad further emphasized the value of knowledge, stating:

"Seeking knowledge is an obligation upon every Muslim." (Sunan Ibn Majah 224)

With such encouragement, Islamic civilization became a beacon of learning, preserving and expanding upon Greek, Persian, Indian, and Chinese knowledge. Scholars from across the Muslim world—from Baghdad to Córdoba—contributed to an unparalleled scientific revolution.

Mathematics: The Birth of Algebra and the Decimal System

Few areas of science have had as profound an impact on human civilization as mathematics, and the contributions of Muslim scholars in this field were revolutionary.

1. Al-Khwarizmi: The Father of Algebra

One of the most celebrated mathematicians of the Islamic Golden Age was Muhammad ibn Musa al-Khwarizmi (c. 780–850 CE). His book, Al-Kitab al-Mukhtasar fi Hisab al-Jabr wal-Muqabala (The Compendious Book on Calculation by Completion and Balancing), laid the foundations of algebra—a term derived from al-Jabr, one of the operations he described.

Al-Khwarizmi's work introduced:

Systematic methods for solving quadratic and linear equations.

The use of symbols for mathematical operations, paving the way for modern algebra.

His contributions were so significant that his name was Latinized as "Algoritmi," giving rise to the modern term "algorithm"—a cornerstone of modern computer science.

2. The Arabic Numerals and the Decimal System

Muslim mathematicians also played a critical role in refining the Hindu-Arabic numeral system, which replaced the cumbersome Roman numerals and became the standard numbering system worldwide.

The use of the decimal system, introduced into Europe through Islamic Spain, allowed for efficient calculation, the development of calculus, and advancements in engineering.

3. Omar Khayyam and the Persian Contribution

The renowned Persian scholar Omar Khayyam (1048–1131 CE), known in the West for his poetry, was also a brilliant mathematician. He contributed to:

The classification of cubic equations and their geometric solutions.

Early foundations of trigonometry, which later influenced European Renaissance scholars.

Through these advancements, Islamic mathematics became the

foundation of modern arithmetic, algebra, and geometry, influencing scientists from Fibonacci to Newton.

Medicine: The Foundations of Modern Healthcare

Islamic medicine was centuries ahead of its time, blending Greek, Persian, and Indian medical traditions while pioneering new discoveries in surgery, pharmacology, and hospital systems.

1. Avicenna (Ibn Sina) and The Canon of Medicine

No discussion of Islamic medicine is complete without mentioning Ibn Sina (Avicenna, 980–1037 CE). His monumental work, Al-Qanun fi al-Tibb (The Canon of Medicine), became the standard medical textbook in Europe for over 500 years. It covered:

Diagnosis and treatment of diseases.

The contagious nature of infections and the need for quarantine (centuries before the discovery of bacteria).

Anatomy, pharmacology, and surgical techniques.

2. Al-Razi (Rhazes) and Smallpox Discovery

Another towering figure in Islamic medicine was Abu Bakr al-Razi (Rhazes, 854–925 CE), who:

Distinguished smallpox from measles for the first time.

Pioneered the use of alcohol in medicine.

Advocated evidence-based medicine, emphasizing clinical trials.

His works influenced both Islamic and European medicine, and his hospital in Baghdad was among the most advanced medical institutions of the medieval world.

3. The Birth of Modern Hospitals

The Islamic hospital system (Bimaristan) was a revolutionary concept, offering:

Specialized wards for different illnesses.

Medical training for students, serving as the forerunners of modern teaching hospitals.

Treatment for all, regardless of wealth or status—an early form of universal healthcare.

Islamic medical advancements directly influenced European medicine, shaping modern healthcare practices.

Astronomy: Mapping the Stars and Navigating the Seas

Islamic civilization made groundbreaking contributions to astronomy, driven by the need to:

Determine prayer times and the direction of the Kaaba (Qibla).

Develop accurate calendars for religious observances.

Advance maritime navigation and exploration.

1. Al-Battani and the Measurement of the Solar Year

The astronomer Al-Battani (858–929 CE) refined the calculations of:

The length of the solar year, improving upon Ptolemaic models.

The positions of planetary orbits, laying the groundwork for Copernican astronomy.

2. Al-Zarqali and the Astrolabe

Al-Zarqali (1029–1087 CE) advanced the astrolabe, an instrument used for:

Navigating the seas, later adopted by European explorers like Columbus.

Calculating prayer times and celestial movements.

3. The Influence on the Renaissance

Many Islamic astronomical texts were later translated into Latin, directly influencing scholars such as Kepler, Copernicus, and Galileo.

Philosophy: The Synthesis of Reason and Revelation

Islamic philosophy, blending Greek rationalism with Islamic theology, led to a golden age of intellectual inquiry.

1. Al-Farabi and Political Philosophy

Al-Farabi (872–950 CE) wrote extensively on the ideal society, influencing medieval political thought.

2. Ibn Rushd (Averroes) and the Defense of Reason

Ibn Rushd (Averroes, 1126–1198 CE) argued that:

Reason and revelation are complementary.

Scientific inquiry is a religious duty.

His works were translated into Latin, influencing Thomas Aquinas and European Scholasticism.

Conclusion: Islam's Scientific Legacy

The contributions of Islamic scientists, mathematicians, and philosophers were instrumental in shaping the modern world. Whether in:

Mathematics (Al-Khwarizmi's algebra, Avicenna's medical advancements).

Astronomy (Al-Battani's planetary calculations, Al-Zarqali's navigation tools).

Medicine (Al-Razi's smallpox discovery, the first hospitals).

Islamic civilization bridged the gap between the ancient and modern worlds.

Although the Islamic Golden Age declined, its knowledge continued to inspire Renaissance Europe and beyond. Today, as we stand in an age of scientific progress, the legacy of Islamic science remains a testament to the power of faith and reason working together—a lesson for future generations.

Islamic Art and Architecture

Calligraphy, mosques, geometric design, and regional styles.

Islamic art and architecture stand as one of the most profound and enduring expressions of the Islamic worldview. Unlike many artistic traditions that emphasize human representation, Islamic art is deeply abstract, geometric, and spiritual, drawing from the core principles of Islamic theology and philosophy. The prohibition of idolatry in Islam led artists to develop unique forms of expression that focus on calligraphy, arabesque patterns, and architectural grandeur, reflecting the unity and transcendence of God (Allah).

From the grand mosques of Istanbul to the intricate tilework of Persia, from the majestic palaces of Andalusia to the symmetrical gardens of Mughal India, Islamic art and architecture have flourished across diverse regions while maintaining a sense of unity, harmony, and divine inspiration.

The Role of Calligraphy in Islamic Art

Perhaps the most distinctive and revered form of Islamic art is calligraphy—the artistic rendering of Arabic script. Because Islam places a central focus on the Qur'an as the word of God, writing became a sacred act, and the transcription of Qur'anic verses developed into an artistic discipline of its own.

1. The Spiritual Significance of Calligraphy

Calligraphy in Islam is not merely a visual art but a spiritual expression, reflecting the beauty and divine essence of the Qur'an. The rhythmic flow of Arabic letters and their stylized elongation create a sense of movement, symbolizing the infinite nature of God. Unlike the human figure, which is absent in religious art, the written word serves as the ultimate representation of divine revelation.

The Qur'an itself emphasizes the power of the written word:

"Read! In the name of your Lord who created." (Surah Al-Alaq, 96:1)

This command to "read" inspired generations of Muslim artists to elevate writing into an art form, adorning mosques, palaces, and manuscripts with intricate inscriptions.

2. Major Styles of Islamic Calligraphy

Over centuries, Muslim calligraphers developed several distinct styles, each with its own aesthetic and historical significance:

Kufic Script: One of the earliest forms of Islamic calligraphy, Kufic is known for its bold, angular letters. It was widely used in early Qur'anic manuscripts and architectural inscriptions, particularly in mosques.

Naskh Script: A more fluid and readable script, Naskh became the preferred style for copying Qur'ans and legal texts.

Thuluth Script: Recognized for its elongated, curved letters, Thuluth is often found in mosque decorations, minarets, and domes.

Diwani Script: Developed in the Ottoman Empire, Diwani is an ornamental and highly stylized script, often used in imperial decrees and court documents.

Maghrebi Script: Found in North Africa and Andalusia, this script has rounded and flowing characters, reflecting the unique artistic influences of the region.

Calligraphy remains a living tradition, continuing to inspire modern artists and designers in the Arab world, Turkey, Iran, and beyond.

The Mosque: The Heart of Islamic Architecture

Islamic architecture is inseparable from the mosque, which serves as the center of worship, learning, and community life. Since the time of Prophet Muhammad, mosques have evolved into architectural masterpieces, reflecting the cultural and artistic traditions of the regions in which they were built.

1. The Evolution of Mosque Architecture

The first mosque in Islam was Masjid al-Nabawi (the Prophet's Mosque) in Medina, built as a simple structure of mud bricks and palm trunks. Over time, as Islamic civilization expanded, mosques became larger and more ornate, incorporating elements such as:

Domes – Symbolizing the vastness of the heavens and the oneness of God.

Minarets – Towers from which the call to prayer (Adhan) is proclaimed.

Mihrabs – A semicircular niche in the wall indicating the direction of Mecca (Qibla).

Courtyards and Fountains – Providing space for congregational gatherings and ablution (wudu).

2. Famous Mosques and Their Architectural Styles

Throughout Islamic history, different regions developed distinct architectural styles, resulting in some of the world's most breathtaking religious monuments.

a) The Great Mosque of Cordoba (Spain)

One of the finest examples of Andalusian architecture, the Great Mosque of Cordoba (built in the 8th century) features horseshoe arches, red-and-white striped columns, and intricate geometric designs.

It reflects the fusion of Islamic and Roman architectural traditions, characteristic of Muslim Spain.

b) The Blue Mosque (Turkey)

The Ottoman architectural masterpiece, the Sultan Ahmed Mosque (Blue Mosque) in Istanbul, is known for its massive dome, towering minarets, and blue-tiled interior.

Ottoman mosques often drew inspiration from Byzantine architecture, particularly the Hagia Sophia.

c) The Alhambra (Spain)

A palace-fortress built by the Nasrid dynasty in Granada, the Alhambra showcases some of the most intricate arabesque patterns and Kufic calligraphy.

Its fountains and courtyards represent the Islamic vision of paradise, echoing the Qur'anic description of gardens with flowing rivers.

d) The Taj Mahal (India)

Built by the Mughal Emperor Shah Jahan, the Taj Mahal is one of the greatest symbols of Islamic art and architecture.

It features a symmetrical white marble structure, floral motifs, and Qur'anic inscriptions.

These structures reflect the diversity and grandeur of Islamic architecture, demonstrating how faith, culture, and aesthetics intertwine.

Geometric Design and Arabesque Patterns

Islamic art is deeply rooted in geometric principles, reflecting the perfection and order of God's creation. Since Islamic theology discourages figurative depictions, artists developed intricate geometric and arabesque designs, symbolizing infinity and divine unity.

1. The Role of Geometry in Islamic Art

Geometric patterns are based on repeating circles, stars, and hexagons, creating an illusion of infinite expansion—a metaphor for the infinite nature of Allah.

This emphasis on mathematical precision was influenced by Islamic advancements in geometry and astronomy.

2. The Arabesque Style

Arabesque patterns consist of interwoven floral and vegetal motifs, symbolizing growth, renewal, and paradise.

They are often found in mosques, palaces, and Qur'anic manuscripts, reinforcing the connection between divine beauty and artistic expression.

3. Islamic Tiles and Mosaics

The use of colored tiles (Zellige in Morocco, Iznik tiles in Turkey) became a hallmark of Islamic architecture, particularly in Persia, Central Asia, and Andalusia.

These mosaics create an aesthetic of harmony and transcendence, transporting the viewer into a spiritual realm.

Conclusion: A Timeless Legacy

Islamic art and architecture embody the spirit of Islamic civilization, blending spirituality, mathematics, and craftsmanship into a timeless aesthetic language. Whether through the graceful strokes of Arabic calligraphy, the celestial domes of mosques, the intricate geometric patterns, or the serene beauty of palace gardens, Islamic artistic expression remains a testament to the faith's enduring pursuit of beauty and divine truth.

Even today, the legacy of Islamic art continues to inspire architects, designers, and artists across the world, proving that art, in its highest form, is a reflection of the divine.

Islam and Society

Role of family, gender relations, and social justice.

Islam is not merely a personal faith—it is a comprehensive way of life that extends into the social, political, and ethical dimensions of human existence. Central to the Islamic worldview is the idea of society as an extension of faith, where individuals live not in isolation but within a network of relationships bound by mutual rights, responsibilities, and moral values.

At the heart of this social structure is the family, which Islam considers the foundation of civilization. Strong family ties ensure the transmission of faith, values, and social stability. Alongside this, Islam offers a structured yet flexible approach to gender relations, promoting equality in spiritual worth while recognizing biological and social differences between men and women. Furthermore, the pursuit of social justice is a fundamental Islamic principle, ensuring that the poor, the marginalized, and the oppressed are cared for.

This chapter explores Islam's vision of society, examining its approach to family life, gender roles, and social justice, demonstrating how these elements work together to create a balanced and ethical civilization.

The Family: The Cornerstone of Islamic Society

Islam views the family as the first and most important unit of society. It is within the family that individuals learn faith, morals, and social responsibilities. The Qur'an describes marriage as a divine blessing, highlighting love, mercy, and companionship as its central components:

"And among His signs is that He created for you spouses from among yourselves so that you may find tranquility in them. And He has placed between you affection and mercy." (Surah Ar-Rum, 30:21)

1. Marriage in Islam

Marriage (Nikah) is not just a legal contract but a sacred covenant in Islam. It is highly encouraged as a means of:

Fostering companionship and emotional support.

Creating a morally upright society.

Providing a stable environment for raising children.

Islamic law places mutual rights and responsibilities upon both spouses:

Men are expected to be providers and protectors of the household.

Women are honored as nurturers and educators of the next generation.

Both spouses must practice kindness, fidelity, and cooperation in marriage.

Marriage is based on mutual consent, and Islam prohibits forced marriages. The Prophet Muhammad explicitly stated:

"A woman should not be married off without her consent." (Sunan Ibn Majah 1873)

2. Parenthood and the Role of Parents

Islam emphasizes respect for parents, particularly mothers, who hold a privileged position due to their sacrifices in childbirth and upbringing. The Prophet Muhammad declared:

"Paradise lies under the feet of your mother." (Sunan an-Nasa'i 3104)

Fathers, on the other hand, bear financial and moral responsibility for their children's education and well-being. Islamic teachings stress parental duty in raising children with good character, faith, and discipline.

3. The Rights of Children

Children in Islam have rights that society must uphold, including:

The right to a good name.

The right to education (both religious and secular).

The right to financial and emotional support.

The Prophet Muhammad was known for his kindness toward children, emphasizing gentle upbringing rather than harsh discipline.

Gender Relations in Islam: A Balance Between Rights and Responsibilities

Islam's approach to gender relations has been widely discussed and often misunderstood. The Qur'an and the Prophet's teachings emphasize that men and women are equal in their spiritual worth, yet they have different but complementary roles in society.

1. Spiritual and Intellectual Equality

The Qur'an explicitly states:

"Indeed, the believing men and believing women are allies of one another. They enjoin what is right and forbid what is wrong." (Surah At-Tawbah, 9:71)

Both men and women are held equally accountable for their actions in this world and the hereafter. Women have historically played key roles as scholars, businesswomen, warriors, and community leaders in Islamic civilization.

2. The Concept of Modesty (Haya')

Islam encourages both men and women to observe modesty in dress, speech, and behavior. The concept of Hijab (modest dressing) applies to both genders, although its form varies across cultures. The Qur'an commands men:

"Tell the believing men to lower their gaze and guard their modesty..." (Surah An-Nur, 24:30)

Likewise, women are also instructed to dress modestly while maintaining their dignity and self-respect.

3. Women's Rights in Islam

Contrary to common misconceptions, Islam granted legal and economic rights to women at a time when such rights were nonexistent in many societies.

The right to education: The Prophet Muhammad said: "Seeking knowledge is obligatory upon every Muslim (male and female)." (Sunan Ibn Majah 224)

The right to own property and conduct business: Khadijah, the Prophet's wife, was a successful merchant.

The right to inheritance: Women have a fixed share in inheritance, as detailed in Surah An-Nisa (4:7-11).

The right to divorce: Islam permits divorce as a last resort when marriage is no longer functional.

While Islamic teachings provide clear guidelines on gender roles, cultural interpretations have sometimes led to misapplications, which should not be mistaken for Islamic principles.

Social Justice in Islam: A Moral Obligation

One of Islam's most defining social principles is the pursuit of justice for all members of society, particularly the poor, the marginalized, and the oppressed.

1. The Obligation of Charity (Zakat and Sadaqah)

Islam mandates that wealth be shared with those in need, emphasizing that economic justice is a duty, not an option.

Zakat: A compulsory charity (2.5% of one's wealth) given annually to the poor.

Sadaqah: Voluntary charity, encouraged at all times.

The Qur'an states:

"And establish prayer and give Zakat, and whatever good you put forward for yourselves—you will find it with Allah." (Surah Al-Baqarah, 2:110)

2. Rights of Workers and Fair Wages

Islam protects labor rights and fair wages, emphasizing that:

"Pay the worker his due before his sweat dries." (Sunan Ibn Majah 2443)

Exploitation of workers and unjust wages are considered oppressive and sinful.

3. Racial Equality and Anti-Discrimination

Islam abolished racial and tribal superiority, emphasizing that piety alone distinguishes individuals. The Prophet Muhammad declared in his final sermon:

"No Arab is superior to a non-Arab, and no white person is superior to a black person, except in piety."

The early Islamic community included diverse ethnic groups, demonstrating a universal brotherhood beyond race or nationality.

Conclusion: Islam's Holistic Vision for Society

Islamic teachings provide a comprehensive framework for a just and balanced society—one that values family stability, gender equity, and social justice. By strengthening family ties, ensuring fair gender relations, and championing the rights of the oppressed, Islam fosters a civilization built on morality, responsibility, and mutual care.

While societies evolve, the core principles of Islam remain timeless, reminding Muslims that faith is not just about personal salvation—it is about creating a world where justice, compassion, and human dignity prevail.

Islamic Economics

Principles of trade, interest (riba), charity (zakat), and Islamic banking.

Islamic economics is an integral part of the broader Islamic way of life, rooted in justice, fairness, and social welfare. Unlike secular economic systems that prioritize profit maximization, Islamic economics is guided by moral and ethical considerations, ensuring that economic activities align with divine principles. It promotes equitable wealth distribution, discourages exploitation, and seeks to create a financial system that benefits all members of society, rather than a privileged few.

At its core, Islamic economics revolves around four key principles:

Trade as a means of lawful wealth generation.

The prohibition of Riba (interest), which leads to financial exploitation.

Charity (Zakat and Sadaqah) as a mechanism for social justice and wealth redistribution.

Islamic banking and finance, which offer Shariah-compliant financial alternatives.

These principles ensure that wealth does not circulate only among the wealthy, but rather benefits the entire community, fulfilling Islam's broader vision of social and economic justice.

Trade in Islam: A Noble Profession

Trade has always held a special status in Islamic civilization. The Prophet Muhammad himself was a merchant, known for his honesty, integrity, and fair dealings in business. The Qur'an encourages lawful trade:

"Allah has permitted trade and has forbidden usury (Riba)." (Surah Al-Baqarah, 2:275)

Islamic trade principles emphasize:

Honesty and transparency in business transactions.

Fair pricing and avoidance of fraud.

Mutual consent between buyers and sellers.

The Prophet Muhammad said:

"The truthful and honest merchant will be with the prophets, the truthful, and the martyrs on the Day of Judgment." (Sunan At-Tirmidhi 1209)

Islamic economics discourages hoarding and speculative trading that create artificial shortages and market instability. Instead, wealth must circulate in the economy, benefiting producers, workers, and consumers alike.

The Prohibition of Riba (Interest): Economic Justice and Stability

One of the most defining features of Islamic economics is the strict prohibition of Riba (interest or usury). The Qur'an strongly condemns interest-based financial transactions, warning of severe consequences for those who engage in them:

"O you who believe! Fear Allah and give up what remains of Riba, if you are believers. But if you do not, then be informed of war from Allah and His Messenger." (Surah Al-Baqarah, 2:278-279)

1. What is Riba?

Riba refers to any guaranteed, fixed increase in a loan or financial transaction, regardless of whether it is small or large. It is prohibited because it:

Creates financial exploitation, benefiting lenders while burdening borrowers.

Leads to economic inequality, concentrating wealth in the hands of a few.

Discourages productive investment, as money is made through

interest rather than trade or innovation.

2. The Islamic Alternative to Interest-Based Financing

In place of Riba, Islam promotes profit-sharing and risk-sharing models such as:

Mudarabah (profit-sharing partnerships): Investors provide capital to entrepreneurs in exchange for a share of profits, with both parties sharing risks and rewards.

Musharakah (joint ventures): Partners contribute capital and expertise to a business, sharing profits based on pre-agreed terms.

These alternatives encourage entrepreneurship, stimulate economic growth, and prevent the concentration of wealth in a few hands.

Zakat and Sadaqah: Wealth Redistribution and Social Justice

Islamic economics is deeply concerned with social justice and the eradication of poverty. One of its most powerful mechanisms for wealth redistribution is Zakat, a compulsory charity that purifies wealth and ensures economic fairness.

1. What is Zakat?

Zakat is an annual obligation upon Muslims who possess wealth above a certain threshold (Nisab). It requires them to give 2.5% of their savings to the poor, orphans, widows, debt-ridden individuals, and other disadvantaged members of society.

The Qur'an states:

"Take from their wealth a charity by which you purify them and cause them to grow." (Surah At-Tawbah, 9:103)

2. Who Receives Zakat?

The Qur'an outlines eight categories of recipients:

The poor (Al-Fuqara) – Those who have no means of income.

The needy (Al-Masakin) – Those who have some wealth but not

enough to sustain themselves.

Those employed to distribute Zakat – Administrators who collect and manage Zakat funds.

New converts to Islam – To strengthen their faith and support their transition.

Those in debt – Individuals burdened by legitimate debts.

Freeing captives – Assisting in the liberation of enslaved people.

Those striving in the cause of Allah – Supporting humanitarian and community welfare projects.

Travelers in distress – Stranded or displaced individuals in need of financial help.

Zakat plays a crucial role in reducing poverty and economic disparity, ensuring that wealth circulates fairly and benefits society as a whole.

3. The Role of Sadaqah (Voluntary Charity)

Beyond Zakat, Islam encourages Sadaqah, voluntary charity that can be given at any time and in any amount. The Prophet Muhammad said:

"Charity does not decrease wealth." (Sahih Muslim 2588)

Sadaqah extends beyond financial giving—it includes acts of kindness, offering help to those in need, and contributing to community welfare.

Islamic Banking and Finance: A Shariah-Compliant Economic Model

With the prohibition of interest-based transactions, modern Islamic banking has developed Shariah-compliant financial solutions that adhere to Islamic principles while meeting contemporary economic needs.

1. The Core Principles of Islamic Banking

Islamic banking operates under three fundamental rules:

No Riba (interest-based earnings).

No Gharar (excessive uncertainty in contracts).

No Haram (forbidden) investments—such as those involving alcohol, gambling, or unethical industries.

2. Key Islamic Financial Products

Islamic banks offer alternative financial instruments based on profit-sharing and ethical investment:

Murabaha (Cost-Plus Financing): Used in home or business financing, where the bank buys an asset and sells it to the customer at an agreed profit margin, rather than charging interest.

Ijara (Leasing Agreements): The bank buys an asset (such as real estate or machinery) and leases it to a customer for a fixed rental fee.

Sukuk (Islamic Bonds): Unlike conventional bonds, which generate interest, Sukuk represents ownership in a tangible asset or project, with profits shared among investors.

Takaful (Islamic Insurance): A cooperative system where members contribute to a mutual fund, avoiding conventional insurance models that involve interest and uncertainty.

Islamic banking has grown rapidly worldwide, with major financial institutions in the Middle East, Southeast Asia, and Europe offering Shariah-compliant banking services.

Conclusion: A Just and Ethical Economic System

Islamic economics presents a balanced, ethical, and socially responsible approach to finance. By promoting fair trade, prohibiting exploitative interest, encouraging charity, and developing Shariah-compliant financial alternatives, it aims to create an economy rooted in justice and social welfare.

Unlike capitalism, which often leads to wealth inequality, and socialism, which can suppress individual enterprise, Islamic economics seeks a middle path, where wealth is earned through lawful trade, shared with the less fortunate, and used for the benefit of society.

At its core, Islamic economics reminds humanity that wealth is a trust from Allah, to be used responsibly for the greater good of all people.

Islamic Governance and Politics

Historical caliphates, political philosophy, and modern governance models.

Islam is not merely a set of theological beliefs or spiritual practices; it is also a comprehensive system that encompasses social order, legal principles, and governance. From the time of Prophet Muhammad (peace be upon him), Islam provided a framework for ruling justly and ethically, ensuring that leadership was tied to moral responsibility, public welfare, and divine guidance.

Throughout history, Islamic governance has taken different forms, from the early caliphates that followed the Prophet to the later empires that ruled vast regions of the world. The core principles of justice, consultation (Shura), accountability, and the rule of law (Shariah) remained central to Islamic political thought. In modern times, Muslims continue to grapple with the role of Islam in governance, as nations debate between Islamic models of governance, secularism, and hybrid systems.

This chapter explores the historical development of Islamic governance, the key philosophical debates surrounding Islamic politics, and contemporary approaches to governing in the modern era.

The Historical Caliphates: Governance After the Prophet

Upon the passing of Prophet Muhammad in 632 CE, the Muslim community was left with the challenge of leadership succession. The Prophet did not leave explicit instructions regarding political leadership, and as a result, early Muslim leaders established a system known as the Caliphate (Khilafah).

The Caliphate was not a hereditary monarchy but rather a political and religious office based on leadership selection. The term Caliph (Khalifah) means "successor", referring to the individual who assumes the role of leading the Muslim community.

1. The Rightly Guided Caliphs (632–661 CE)

The first four caliphs—Abu Bakr, Umar, Uthman, and Ali—are known as the Rightly Guided Caliphs (Al-Khulafa' Al-Rashidun) because they ruled according to Islamic principles of justice, consultation, and piety.

Abu Bakr (632–634 CE): The first caliph, chosen through Shura (consultation), who unified Arabia under Islam.

Umar ibn al-Khattab (634–644 CE): Expanded the Islamic empire and established administrative and judicial reforms.

Uthman ibn Affan (644–656 CE): Standardized the Qur'anic text but faced political opposition leading to his assassination.

Ali ibn Abi Talib (656–661 CE): His rule was marked by civil strife, leading to the first major split in Islam between Sunni and Shi'a factions.

This period is often viewed as the golden age of Islamic governance, where leadership was accountable to the people and based on Islamic ethics.

2. The Umayyad and Abbasid Dynasties

As Islam expanded, governance became more complex, leading to the establishment of dynastic rule.

The Umayyads (661–750 CE): Established by Mu'awiyah I, the Umayyads transformed the caliphate into a more centralized monarchy, with Damascus as its capital. While they expanded the empire from Spain to Central Asia, they faced criticism for favoring Arab elites over non-Arabs.

The Abbasids (750–1258 CE): Overthrew the Umayyads and established Baghdad as a cultural and intellectual center, fostering advances in science, philosophy, and governance.

The Abbasid era saw the development of a bureaucratic state, where Islamic scholars (Ulama) played a larger role in shaping governance through legal and ethical interpretations of Shariah.

3. Later Islamic Empires and Political Structures

Following the decline of the Abbasids, various Islamic empires emerged, each implementing governance according to their own interpretations of Islamic principles:

The Ottoman Empire (1299–1924): One of the longest-lasting Islamic empires, with the Sultan-Caliph model, where the ruler was both a political and religious leader.

The Mughal Empire (1526–1857): A powerful Indian empire that blended Islamic governance with Persian and Indian traditions.

The Safavid Empire (1501–1736): Established Shi'a Islam as the state religion in Persia, influencing modern Iranian governance.

These empires adapted Islamic principles to different cultural and political environments, demonstrating the flexibility of Islamic governance.

Islamic Political Philosophy: Key Debates and Principles

Islamic political thought has historically revolved around three major questions:

What is the ideal form of governance in Islam?

What is the role of religious authority in politics?

How should justice be implemented in an Islamic state?

1. The Role of Shura (Consultation) and Leadership Accountability

The Qur'an mandates consultation (Shura) in governance, stating:

"And those who have responded to [the call of] their sovereign, establish prayer, and whose affairs are [determined by] consultation among themselves." (Surah Ash-Shura, 42:38)

This principle suggests that rulers must consult the people in decision-making. Classical scholars debated whether this meant a democratic selection of leaders or an advisory council within an Islamic framework.

2. The Balance Between Religious and Political Authority

Islam does not separate religion and governance in the way modern secular systems do. However, the degree of religious involvement in governance has varied across Islamic history:

Al-Farabi (872–950 CE): Advocated for a philosopher-king who governs with wisdom and virtue.

Al-Mawardi (972–1058 CE): Defined the role of the Caliph as both a religious and political leader, arguing that rulers must uphold Islamic law.

Ibn Khaldun (1332–1406 CE): Developed a theory of political cycles, stating that dynasties rise and fall due to moral and social decay.

These scholars shaped Islamic political thought, influencing later governance models.

Modern Islamic Governance: Between Tradition and Reform

In the modern era, Muslim-majority nations have developed different governance models, ranging from Islamic states to secular republics.

1. Theocracy vs. Secularism in the Muslim World

Iran (Islamic Republic): A Shi'a theocracy where religious scholars (Ayatollahs) wield significant power.

Saudi Arabia (Monarchical Islamic State): A monarchy that enforces Shariah law, but with an authoritarian political structure.

Turkey (Secular Republic): Founded by Atatürk as a secular state, but with an increasing role for Islam in governance.

2. The Rise of Islamic Democracy

Some nations, like Malaysia, Indonesia, and Tunisia, have developed hybrid models, integrating Islamic values with democratic governance. These systems attempt to:

Uphold Islamic principles while ensuring political participation.

Allow religious law to coexist with modern legal frameworks.

The question of how Islam interacts with democracy and human rights continues to be debated among scholars and policymakers.

Conclusion: The Future of Islamic Governance

Islamic governance has evolved from the early Caliphate to modern nation-states, reflecting changing political, economic, and social realities. While justice, consultation, and accountability remain central to Islamic political philosophy, different nations interpret these principles in diverse ways.

In the 21st century, the debate over Islam's role in governance remains highly relevant. Some advocate for a return to Islamic principles in politics, while others seek to reconcile Islam with modern democratic ideals. The challenge ahead is to develop governance models that uphold Islamic ethics while ensuring justice, human rights, and social welfare for all citizens.

Regardless of form, the ultimate goal of Islamic governance remains the same: to create a just, moral, and prosperous society guided by divine principles.

Sunni Islam: The Majority Tradition

Beliefs, jurisprudence, and key theological perspectives.

Sunni Islam represents the largest branch of Islam, encompassing approximately 85-90% of the global Muslim population. Rooted in the foundational teachings of the Qur'an and the Sunnah (the prophetic tradition), Sunni Islam developed as the dominant tradition following the passing of Prophet Muhammad (peace be upon him). It is characterized by its adherence to the early consensus of the Muslim community (Ijma'), its recognition of the first four Caliphs as rightful leaders, and its structured system of jurisprudence and theology.

Sunni Islam is not a monolithic entity—it includes various schools of law, theology, and spiritual thought, yet all share a core commitment to the fundamental principles of Islam as taught by Prophet Muhammad. This chapter explores the beliefs, legal traditions, and theological perspectives of Sunni Islam, offering a deeper understanding of what defines the majority tradition of the Muslim world.

Core Beliefs of Sunni Islam

Sunni Muslims adhere to the Articles of Faith (Iman), which constitute the essential beliefs of Islam. These include:

Tawhid (Oneness of God): The absolute belief in Allah's oneness, rejecting any form of polytheism or association with the divine (Shirk).

Belief in Angels: Acknowledging that angels are created by Allah to fulfill divine commands.

Belief in the Divine Scriptures: Recognizing the Qur'an as the final revelation, while affirming the validity of earlier scriptures (Torah, Psalms, Gospel) in their original forms.

Belief in Prophets: Accepting that Allah sent prophets to guide humanity, with Prophet Muhammad as the final and seal of all prophets (Khatam an-Nabiyyin).

Belief in the Day of Judgment: The certainty of resurrection, accountability, and eternal reward or punishment in the Hereafter.

Belief in Divine Decree (Qadr): Understanding that everything occurs by Allah's will and knowledge, balancing human free will with divine predestination.

These beliefs unite all Sunni Muslims, forming the theological foundation of Sunni Islam's worldview.

Sunni Jurisprudence (Fiqh): The Four Schools of Law

Sunni Islam is diverse in its legal interpretations, but it remains unified in its sources of law—the Qur'an, the Sunnah, Ijma' (consensus), and Qiyas (analogy). This legal framework led to the emergence of four major Sunni schools of jurisprudence, each named after its founding scholar.

1. The Hanafi School

Founder: Imam Abu Hanifa (699–767 CE).

Key Features:

The most flexible and rationalist school, giving greater emphasis to analogy (Qiyas) and juristic preference (Istihsan).

Widely followed in Turkey, Central Asia, the Indian subcontinent, and parts of the Middle East.

2. The Maliki School

Founder: Imam Malik ibn Anas (711–795 CE).

Key Features:

Emphasizes the practice of the people of Medina, considering their customs as an authentic representation of Prophetic practice.

Predominantly followed in North Africa, West Africa, and parts of the Arabian Peninsula.

3. The Shafi'i School

Founder: Imam Al-Shafi'i (767–820 CE).

Key Features:

Places equal importance on the Qur'an and Hadith as primary sources of law.

Strong influence in Egypt, Indonesia, Malaysia, and the Horn of Africa.

4. The Hanbali School

Founder: Imam Ahmad ibn Hanbal (780–855 CE).

Key Features:

The most textually strict school, prioritizing Hadith over personal reasoning.

Primarily followed in Saudi Arabia and parts of the Gulf region.

Despite their differences in methodology, all four Sunni schools are considered valid and respected interpretations of Islamic law, with scholars from each tradition recognizing the legitimacy of the others.

Sunni Theological Schools: Understanding the Nature of God and Faith

Over the centuries, Sunni theology has been shaped by three major theological schools, each offering distinct perspectives on the nature of God, divine attributes, and human reason.

1. The Ash'ari School

Founder: Imam Abu al-Hasan al-Ash'ari (873–936 CE).

Key Beliefs:

Reconciles reason and revelation, asserting that divine attributes should be accepted without human interpretation (bila kayf – "without asking how").

Holds that good and evil are determined by divine will, not by human reasoning alone.

Influence: The dominant theology in North Africa, the Middle East, and parts of the Indian subcontinent.

2. The Maturidi School

Founder: Imam Abu Mansur al-Maturidi (853–944 CE).

Key Beliefs:

Places greater emphasis on human reason while still affirming the authority of divine revelation.

Believes that humans can recognize moral truths independently, but divine revelation provides complete guidance.

Influence: Strong in Central Asia, Turkey, and parts of South Asia.

3. The Salafi (or Athari) School

Key Figures: Early scholars like Ahmad ibn Hanbal, and later proponents like Ibn Taymiyyah.

Key Beliefs:

Rejects theological speculation and philosophical reasoning, adhering to a literal interpretation of divine attributes.

Avoids allegorical explanations, relying on the Qur'an and Hadith without rational speculation.

Influence: Primarily found in Saudi Arabia and parts of the Gulf region.

These theological schools reflect different approaches to understanding Islam while remaining within the broader Sunni tradition.

Sunni Islam in the Modern World

As the largest branch of Islam, Sunni Muslims live across diverse cultures, languages, and political systems. Sunni-majority nations include Egypt, Turkey, Saudi Arabia, Indonesia, Pakistan, and Morocco, among others.

Despite regional differences, Sunni Islam continues to emphasize:

Adherence to the Qur'an and Sunnah as the primary sources of guidance.

Legal plurality, allowing for multiple interpretations while maintaining unity.

Engagement with contemporary challenges, such as governance, technology, and interfaith relations.

In modern times, Sunni scholars continue to interpret Islamic teachings in response to globalization, human rights, and modern political structures. Institutions like Al-Azhar University in Egypt and Darul Uloom in South Asia remain influential in shaping Sunni thought.

Conclusion: The Strength and Diversity of Sunni Islam

Sunni Islam, as the majority tradition of the Muslim world, has maintained a balance between faith, law, and theology, allowing for both unity and diversity. Whether in its legal schools, theological traditions, or modern interpretations, Sunni Islam remains deeply rooted in the Qur'an and the Sunnah, while adapting to changing times.

Despite regional and doctrinal differences, Sunni Islam has endured as a dynamic and resilient tradition, shaping the religious, intellectual, and cultural life of the Muslim world. Its legacy continues to guide millions toward a deeper understanding of faith, morality, and divine purpose.

Shi'a Islam: Origins and Beliefs

Theological differences, sects (Twelver, Ismaili, Zaydi), and leadership doctrines.

Islam, from its earliest days, was marked by a deep sense of unity, as its followers adhered to the teachings of Prophet Muhammad (peace be upon him). However, following the Prophet's passing in 632 CE, questions surrounding leadership and succession led to differing interpretations among his followers. The division that emerged between the Sunni and Shi'a branches of Islam is rooted primarily in disagreements over leadership, but over time, it also evolved into theological, jurisprudential, and cultural differences.

Shi'a Islam, representing approximately 10-15% of the global Muslim population, is the second-largest branch of Islam, with its most significant presence in Iran, Iraq, Lebanon, Bahrain, and parts of Yemen, Pakistan, and India. While Shi'a and Sunni Muslims share the fundamental beliefs of Islam, such as the oneness of God (Tawhid), belief in the Qur'an, and the prophethood of Muhammad, the Shi'a tradition has distinct beliefs regarding leadership (Imamate), theology, and spiritual authority.

This chapter explores the origins of Shi'a Islam, its key theological differences from Sunni Islam, its major sects (Twelver, Ismaili, and Zaydi), and the concept of the Imamate, which is central to Shi'a identity.

Origins of Shi'a Islam: The Question of Leadership

The term "Shi'a" comes from the Arabic Shi'at Ali, meaning "the party of Ali". It refers to those who believed that leadership of the Muslim community should have remained within the family of the Prophet Muhammad, specifically through his cousin and son-in-law, Ali ibn Abi Talib.

1. The Dispute Over Succession

After the Prophet's death, a group of Muslims—who would later be identified as Sunnis—believed that leadership should be determined through consultation (Shura) and consensus. As a result, Abu Bakr, a close companion of the Prophet, was chosen as the first Caliph.

However, another group of Muslims—who would later form the Shi'a tradition—argued that Ali was divinely appointed by the Prophet Muhammad at Ghadir Khumm, an event where the Prophet reportedly said:

"For whomever I am his Mawla (guardian/leader), then Ali is also his Mawla." (Hadith reported in Sunni and Shi'a sources)

Shi'a Muslims interpret this statement as a clear designation of Ali as the rightful successor, whereas Sunnis see it as an expression of respect and spiritual closeness, not political leadership.

Ali eventually became the fourth Caliph (656–661 CE) but was assassinated during the internal conflicts that followed. His son, Husayn ibn Ali, became the focal point of Shi'a identity when he was martyred in the Battle of Karbala in 680 CE by the forces of the Umayyad Caliphate. This event became a defining moment in Shi'a history, symbolizing resistance against oppression and a commitment to justice.

Theological Differences Between Sunni and Shi'a Islam

While both Sunni and Shi'a Islam share core Islamic beliefs, three key theological differences distinguish them:

1. The Imamate vs. the Caliphate

Sunni Islam holds that leadership is a political matter, with Caliphs chosen through consultation or selection by leaders of the Muslim community.

Shi'a Islam believes that leadership is a divine appointment. The rightful leaders of the Muslim community are Imams, who are descendants of the Prophet Muhammad through Ali and Fatimah (the Prophet's daughter).

Shi'a Muslims believe that these Imams are infallible (Ma'sūm) and possess divinely granted knowledge.

2. The Role of the Imams

Shi'a theology views the Imams as more than political rulers; they are spiritual guides and sources of divine wisdom, similar to how prophets were in previous generations.

The Twelver Shi'a believe in a lineage of 12 divinely appointed Imams, ending with the Mahdi, the hidden Imam who will return as a savior.

Sunnis, in contrast, do not assign infallibility or divine authority to any leader after Prophet Muhammad.

3. The Concept of Martyrdom and Justice

The martyrdom of Husayn at Karbala is a central theme in Shi'a spirituality. It represents the struggle against tyranny and is commemorated every year during Ashura, a day of mourning and reflection. Shi'a Muslims place strong emphasis on standing against injustice and awaiting the return of the Mahdi, who will restore justice to the world.

The Major Sects of Shi'a Islam

Over time, Shi'a Islam itself developed into several sects based on differences over leadership and theological interpretations. The three major sects are:

1. Twelver Shi'a (Ithna Ashariyah) – The Largest Group

Followers believe in 12 Imams, beginning with Ali and ending with Imam Muhammad al-Mahdi, who is believed to be in occultation (Ghaybah) and will return as the Mahdi (the Guided One) to restore justice.

Twelvers believe in the role of scholars (Ayatollahs) as representatives of the hidden Imam, guiding the community in religious matters.

Dominant in Iran, Iraq, Lebanon, and Bahrain.

2. Ismaili Shi'a – The Philosophical Tradition

Belief in a continuing, living Imam rather than a hidden one. The current Ismaili Imam is Aga Khan IV.

Strong emphasis on philosophy, mysticism, and esoteric interpretations of Islam.

Historically played a major role in the Fatimid Caliphate (10th-12th century).

Found in India, Pakistan, East Africa, and parts of Central Asia.

3. Zaydi Shi'a – The Political Tradition

Recognize only five Imams, starting from Ali and his descendants.

Unlike Twelvers, Zaydis do not believe in the infallibility of the Imams.

Emphasize active resistance and leadership through merit, rather than divine appointment.

Found primarily in Yemen, where they have had a long political history.

Shi'a Islam in the Modern World

Shi'a Islam has played a significant role in the modern Islamic world.

The Iranian Revolution (1979) established the first modern Shi'a Islamic Republic, where religious leaders (Ayatollahs) wield political authority.

Shi'a communities in Iraq, Lebanon, and Yemen have been deeply involved in political and sectarian conflicts due to historical tensions with Sunni governments.

Despite political divisions, Shi'a and Sunni Muslims share daily religious practices, pilgrimage sites (Mecca and Medina), and interfaith dialogues to foster unity.

Conclusion: Shi'a Islam's Enduring Legacy

Shi'a Islam remains a vibrant and diverse tradition, with deep theological roots and a powerful historical legacy. Despite its differences with Sunni Islam, it shares the essential pillars of Islamic faith and continues to be an influential force in Islamic thought, politics, and spirituality.

At its heart, Shi'a Islam emphasizes justice, divine leadership, and the struggle against oppression, values that have inspired millions of Muslims throughout history. Whether in the form of Twelver belief in the awaited Mahdi, Ismaili philosophical thought, or Zaydi political activism, Shi'a Islam continues to shape the spiritual and intellectual landscape of the Muslim world.

Other Islamic Sects and Movements

Kharijites, Ahmadiyya, Ibadiyya, Salafism, and modern reform movements.

Islamic history has been marked by diverse interpretations, movements, and sects that have shaped the religious, political, and social landscape of the Muslim world. While Sunni and Shi'a Islam form the two largest branches, other groups have emerged over time, often as a response to theological, political, or societal challenges. Some of these groups developed alternative doctrinal positions, while others represented revivalist or reformist efforts within mainstream Islam.

Among the most historically significant and influential movements are the Kharijites, Ahmadiyya, Ibadiyya, Salafism, and modern reform movements. Each of these sects or movements has contributed uniquely to the evolution of Islamic thought, whether by challenging established religious authorities, redefining governance, or advocating for revival and reform.

This chapter explores the origins, beliefs, and impact of these groups, shedding light on their role in the broader Islamic tradition.

The Kharijites: The First Sectarian Split in Islam

The Kharijites (Khawarij) were the first sect to emerge in Islam, forming in the aftermath of the Battle of Siffin (657 CE)—a conflict between Ali ibn Abi Talib, the fourth Caliph, and Mu'awiyah, the governor of Syria. The dispute revolved around leadership and arbitration, and when Ali agreed to settle the matter through negotiation, a faction of his followers revolted against him, arguing that only God has the right to decide leadership, not human arbitration.

1. Core Beliefs of the Kharijites

They held an extreme view of piety, believing that any Muslim who commits a major sin ceases to be a Muslim and can be justifiably fought against.

They rejected the idea of dynastic or hereditary leadership, arguing that the most righteous individual—regardless of lineage—should be the leader of the Muslim community.

They practiced takfir, the act of excommunicating other Muslims, which later influenced extremist ideologies in some factions.

2. The Decline of the Kharijites

Over time, the Kharijites engaged in violent uprisings against both Sunni and Shi'a rulers, believing that those who did not adhere to their strict interpretation of Islam were apostates. Their radical stance led to their marginalization, though some of their ideological remnants persisted in later extremist movements.

Ibadiyya: The Moderate Offshoot of the Kharijites

Unlike the extremist Kharijites, the Ibadiyya developed into a more moderate sect, establishing a distinct theological and political tradition. The Ibadis are primarily found in Oman, parts of North Africa (Libya, Algeria, and Tunisia), and East Africa.

1. Key Beliefs of the Ibadis

Like the Kharijites, they believe that leadership should be based on piety and merit, not lineage.

Unlike the Kharijites, they do not practice violent takfir, choosing to distance themselves peacefully from those they consider misguided rather than excommunicating them.

They emphasize justice, simplicity, and communal decision-making, preferring a council-based leadership rather than monarchy or dynastic rule.

2. The Ibadi Political System: The Imamate

In Oman, the Ibadi Imamate persisted for centuries, emphasizing a consultative and religiously guided political structure. Even today, Oman remains the only country with an Ibadi-majority population, influencing its unique approach to governance and diplomacy.

Ahmadiyya: A Controversial Modern Sect

The Ahmadiyya movement was founded in the late 19th century in British India by Mirza Ghulam Ahmad (1835–1908), who claimed to be the Mahdi and Messiah—a role traditionally believed to be fulfilled in the end times. This claim led to significant theological controversy, with both Sunni and Shi'a scholars rejecting his prophethood.

1. Core Beliefs of Ahmadiyya

They believe that Mirza Ghulam Ahmad was divinely appointed as a reformer and Messiah, sent to revive Islam.

They emphasize non-violence, religious tolerance, and the separation of religion from politics.

They believe that Jesus (Isa) did not ascend to heaven but instead died a natural death, differing from mainstream Islamic eschatology.

2. The Persecution of Ahmadis

Ahmadis are considered heretical by most Muslim scholars, and in some countries, such as Pakistan and Saudi Arabia, they are officially declared non-Muslims. They face legal restrictions and social discrimination, particularly in South Asia and parts of the Middle East.

Despite opposition, the Ahmadiyya community has established global outreach programs, humanitarian efforts, and educational institutions in countries such as the UK, Canada, and the USA.

Salafism: A Return to the Early Islamic Practices

Salafism is not a sect in the traditional sense but rather a revivalist movement that seeks to return to the practices of the early Muslims (Salaf as-Salih). It emerged as a response to what its followers saw as religious innovations (Bid'ah) and cultural deviations from pure Islam.

1. Core Beliefs of Salafism

Salafis emphasize a literal interpretation of the Qur'an and Hadith, rejecting philosophical and mystical interpretations.

They reject sectarian divisions, claiming to follow pure Islam as practiced by the early generations.

They oppose the veneration of saints, shrines, and Sufi practices, considering them un-Islamic innovations.

2. The Political Variants of Salafism

Salafism has different strands, ranging from quietist Salafis, who focus only on personal piety, to political Salafis, who advocate for implementing Islamic governance.

Wahhabism, a subset of Salafism founded by Muhammad ibn Abd al-Wahhab (1703–1792) in Arabia, became the dominant ideology of Saudi Arabia, influencing modern Islamic thought and law.

Some extremist factions, such as al-Qaeda and ISIS, have distorted Salafi teachings to justify political violence, although mainstream Salafis strongly condemn terrorism.

Modern Islamic Reform Movements

In addition to traditional sects, modern reform movements have sought to reinterpret Islam in light of contemporary challenges, addressing issues such as colonialism, modernity, democracy, and human rights.

1. The Islamic Modernism Movement

Figures like Jamal al-Din al-Afghani (1838–1897) and Muhammad Abduh (1849–1905) called for reform in Islamic thought, arguing that Islam must adapt to modern science, governance, and education.

2. The Muslim Brotherhood

Founded in 1928 in Egypt by Hassan al-Banna, the Muslim Brotherhood sought to restore Islamic governance while using modern political structures. It remains one of the most influential Islamic political movements today.

3. Liberal Islam

Some Muslim intellectuals advocate for a progressive approach, promoting gender equality, human rights, and interfaith dialogue while maintaining Islamic principles. This movement, however, faces opposition from conservative scholars who argue that it compromises Islamic teachings.

Conclusion: The Diversity of Islamic Thought

Islam is a diverse and dynamic tradition, with different sects and movements shaping its historical and contemporary landscape. From the political activism of the Kharijites, to the theological disputes surrounding Ahmadiyya, to the Salafi revivalist efforts, each movement reflects a unique response to the challenges faced by the Muslim community.

Despite theological differences, these sects and movements continue to influence the political, social, and intellectual discourse of the Muslim world, demonstrating that Islamic thought is not static, but ever-evolving in its engagement with history and modernity.

The Spread of Islam: A Historical Overview

Expansion from Arabia to Africa, Asia, and Europe.

The story of Islam's expansion is one of the most remarkable in world history. Within a century of its inception, Islam grew from a small religious movement in the deserts of Arabia to a dominant force spanning multiple continents. What began with a single revelation to the Prophet Muhammad (peace be upon him) in the early 7th century soon transformed into a global civilization.

Islam's spread was not solely a military or political endeavor; it was a process shaped by trade, diplomacy, religious teachings, and cultural exchange. From the Arabian Peninsula, Islam reached North Africa, the Middle East, Central and South Asia, and even parts of Europe, influencing societies, reshaping governance, and leaving an enduring impact on human history.

This chapter explores the historical phases of Islam's expansion, the key figures and dynasties that played a role, and the various methods—military, economic, and intellectual—through which Islam spread across the world.

The Early Expansion (622–750 CE): From Arabia to a Global Empire

Islam's spread began with Prophet Muhammad's mission in Mecca and his migration (Hijrah) to Medina in 622 CE. During his lifetime, Islam gained followers through both peaceful preaching and defensive battles. By the time of his passing in 632 CE, most of the Arabian Peninsula had embraced Islam.

1. The Rashidun Caliphate (632–661 CE): Conquest and Consolidation

Following the Prophet's death, leadership passed to the first four Caliphs, known as the Rightly Guided Caliphs (Al-Khulafa' Al-Rashidun): Abu Bakr, Umar, Uthman, and Ali.

Under their rule, Islam expanded rapidly into the Byzantine and Sassanian empires, the two superpowers of the time. The reasons for this success included:

Discontent within the Byzantine and Persian empires, which were weakened by internal strife and heavy taxation.

The appeal of Islamic governance, which introduced a system of justice, lower taxes, and protection for religious minorities.

The dedication of Muslim armies, who were driven by both faith and the promise of a better socio-political order.

Key conquests included:

The Levant and Syria (636 CE): The decisive Battle of Yarmouk led to the Muslim conquest of Damascus and Jerusalem.

Persia (637–651 CE): The defeat of the powerful Sassanian Empire at the Battle of Qadisiyyah led to the Islamization of Iran.

Egypt (641 CE): The Muslim commander Amr ibn al-As captured Alexandria, bringing Islam to North Africa.

2. The Umayyad Caliphate (661–750 CE): The Golden Age of Expansion

Under the Umayyads, Islam expanded at an unprecedented rate, reaching Spain in the West and Central Asia in the East.

North Africa and the Maghreb: The conquest of modern-day Algeria, Tunisia, and Morocco led to Islam's spread among the Berber tribes, many of whom later played a key role in further expansion.

Spain (Al-Andalus, 711 CE): Led by Tariq ibn Ziyad, Muslim forces crossed the Strait of Gibraltar and defeated the Visigothic kingdom, establishing Islamic rule in Spain that would last for nearly 800 years.

Central Asia: Muslim armies reached the borders of China by 751 CE, bringing Islam to modern-day Uzbekistan, Turkmenistan, and Afghanistan.

The Umayyads governed one of the largest empires in history, and while conquests played a role in spreading Islam, many non-Arabs initially retained their own religious beliefs. Over time, Islam spread through intermarriage, trade, and governance, leading to widespread conversion.

The Abbasid Era (750–1258 CE): The Spread of Islamic Civilization

The Abbasid Caliphate, which overthrew the Umayyads in 750 CE, shifted the focus from conquest to cultural and intellectual expansion.

Baghdad became a center of learning, home to the House of Wisdom (Bayt al-Hikma), where scholars translated Greek, Persian, and Indian texts, leading to advances in mathematics, medicine, and astronomy.

Islam spread peacefully through trade, especially in West Africa, India, and Southeast Asia, where merchants introduced Islamic teachings.

Despite the Mongol destruction of Baghdad in 1258, Islam's intellectual and religious influence continued to grow.

Islam's Spread to Africa, Asia, and Europe

While the early Caliphates expanded Islam through conquest, in later centuries, Islam spread through trade, missionaries (Sufis), and diplomacy.

1. Islam in Africa

Islam reached Africa through both conquest and trade.

North Africa: Islam became deeply rooted under the Umayyads and Abbasids. Cities like Cairo and Fez became centers of learning.

West Africa: Islam spread through the trans-Saharan trade routes, leading to the rise of Islamic kingdoms like Mali and Songhai.

East Africa: Arab and Persian traders introduced Islam to the Swahili Coast (Kenya, Tanzania, Zanzibar), blending with local cultures.

2. Islam in the Indian Subcontinent

The first Muslim incursions into Sindh (modern Pakistan) occurred in 711 CE, led by Muhammad bin Qasim.

Over time, Islam spread through Sufi missionaries, merchants, and later, the Delhi Sultanate (1206–1526 CE) and the Mughal Empire (1526–1857 CE).

Millions of Hindus and Buddhists converted, particularly in regions that are now Pakistan, Bangladesh, and parts of India.

3. Islam in Southeast Asia

Unlike in many other regions, Islam spread peacefully in Southeast Asia, primarily through trade and Sufi missionary efforts.

Indonesia, Malaysia, and the Philippines saw gradual conversions between the 13th and 16th centuries, influenced by Muslim traders from India, Persia, and the Arabian Peninsula.

Today, Indonesia is the world's largest Muslim-majority country, a testament to Islam's non-military spread.

4. Islam in Europe

Islamic rule in Spain (Al-Andalus) fostered a golden age of science, philosophy, and interfaith cooperation. However, by 1492, the Catholic monarchs expelled Muslims following the fall of Granada.

Ottoman Expansion: From the 14th to 17th centuries, the Ottoman Empire spread Islam into the Balkans, Greece, Hungary, and parts of Eastern Europe.

Today, Islam remains the second-largest religion in Europe, with historical communities in Bosnia, Albania, and Turkey, as well as newer immigrant communities.

Conclusion: A Civilization That Continues to Grow

Islam's spread across the world is a testament to its adaptability and universality. While early expansions involved military conquests, Islam's long-term influence has come through trade, scholarship, and spiritual movements.

Today, Islam is one of the fastest-growing religions, with over 1.9 billion adherents worldwide. From the deserts of Arabia to the islands of Indonesia, from the palaces of Cordoba to the mosques of Istanbul, Islam's influence remains deeply embedded in the fabric of global history.

This expansion was not merely about political control; it was about building civilizations, sharing knowledge, and transforming societies—a process that continues in the modern world today.

Islam in the Modern World

Challenges, contemporary issues, and Islam's interaction with modernity.

Islam, one of the world's largest and most influential religions, continues to shape the lives of over 1.9 billion people across the globe. While deeply rooted in tradition, faith, and scripture, Islam also finds itself in constant interaction with the challenges of modernity, globalization, political shifts, and evolving societal norms. The modern world presents both opportunities and obstacles for Muslims—whether in governance, education, technology, human rights, or interfaith dialogue.

The 21st century has witnessed significant debates surrounding Islam's role in public life, its place in secular societies, and its response to contemporary challenges. From technological advancements to geopolitical conflicts, from Muslim identity in the West to the revival of Islamic scholarship, the relationship between Islam and modernity remains complex and evolving.

This chapter explores some of the major challenges and contemporary issues facing Islam today, as well as how Muslims and Islamic institutions are adapting to an ever-changing world.

1. Islam and Globalization: Opportunities and Struggles

In the past, the spread of Islam occurred through trade, scholarship, and conquest. Today, it is influenced by globalization, media, and digital communication.

The Internet and Social Media: Platforms like YouTube, Twitter, and Facebook have allowed Muslim scholars, thinkers, and influencers to disseminate Islamic knowledge, while also exposing Islam to misrepresentation and misinformation.

The Role of Muslim Diasporas: Large Muslim communities in Europe, North America, and Australia face the challenge of maintaining religious identity while integrating into secular, multicultural societies.

Islamic Finance and Economics: The emergence of Islamic banking and ethical finance has provided Muslims with financial models that align with Shariah principles, proving that Islam can adapt to modern economic systems.

However, globalization has also created cultural and ideological tensions, particularly in how Islamic values interact with Western secular norms, human rights, and gender roles.

2. The Question of Islam and Secularism

The relationship between religion and the state has been a major debate in the modern Muslim world.

Secular Muslim-majority countries like Turkey and Tunisia have sought to limit Islam's role in politics, leading to tensions between religious and secular groups.

Islamic republics, such as Iran and Pakistan, aim to blend Islam with governance, but often face challenges regarding human rights, democracy, and political freedoms.

The Arab Spring (2010-2012) demonstrated a popular demand for political reform, but also revealed the fragility of governance models that attempt to balance Islamic values with democracy.

The question remains: Can Islam coexist with secular governance while maintaining its spiritual and ethical foundations? This debate continues to shape legal, political, and cultural discussions in Muslim-majority nations.

3. Islam, Human Rights, and Women's Rights

The issue of human rights in Islam is often debated, particularly in areas such as freedom of speech, gender equality, and minority rights.

Women's Roles in Society: Many Muslim-majority countries are seeing a rise in women's education, workforce participation, and leadership roles. However, there are ongoing discussions on dress codes, legal rights, and religious freedoms.

Religious Minorities: Non-Muslims in Muslim-majority nations sometimes face legal restrictions, while Muslim minorities in non-Muslim countries deal with discrimination and Islamophobia.

Freedom of Expression vs. Blasphemy Laws: Some Muslim-majority countries criminalize blasphemy, while others advocate for freedom of thought within an Islamic framework.

The question of balancing Islamic law with universal human rights is an ongoing challenge that scholars, policymakers, and activists continue to address.

4. Islam and Science: A Renewed Engagement?

Throughout history, Islam played a pivotal role in scientific and philosophical advancements. However, in the modern era, the relationship between Islam and science has faced setbacks due to colonialism, political instability, and educational stagnation.

Revival of Islamic Scholarship: Universities and institutions in Muslim-majority countries are now focusing on STEM (Science, Technology, Engineering, and Mathematics) education, inspired by Islam's golden age of scientific inquiry.

Medical Ethics and Islamic Bioethics: Issues such as organ donation, genetic engineering, and artificial intelligence are being addressed within an Islamic ethical framework.

Environmentalism and Islam: Many contemporary Muslim scholars are reinterpreting Qur'anic teachings on nature to emphasize sustainability, conservation, and climate action.

A renewed engagement with scientific inquiry and ethical technological advancements is seen as a way to integrate Islam into modernity without abandoning its core principles.

5. Islamophobia and the Struggles of Muslim Minorities

In Western societies, Muslims often face discrimination, surveillance, and stereotyping, particularly in the aftermath of terrorist attacks falsely associated with Islam.

Hate crimes and discrimination: In countries like the USA, UK, France, and India, anti-Muslim rhetoric has risen, sometimes leading to hate crimes, hijab bans, and racial profiling.

Media Portrayal: Western media often frames Islam through the lens of terrorism and extremism, reinforcing negative stereotypes.

Interfaith Initiatives: Many Muslim leaders and communities are engaging in dialogue with Christians, Jews, and other faith groups to promote understanding and cooperation.

Despite these challenges, Muslims in Europe and North America are becoming politically active, contributing to academia, arts, and sciences, and shaping the future of Islam in pluralistic societies.

6. The Future of Islam in the Modern World

Despite political conflicts and ideological debates, Islam remains one of the fastest-growing religions worldwide, with conversions, birthrates, and global migration contributing to its expansion.

Key Trends in the Future of Islam:

Digital Islam: Online scholars, virtual learning, and Islamic apps are making religious education more accessible and personalized.

Islamic Political Thought: The balance between Shariah and democracy will continue to evolve in countries that seek both modern governance and religious values.

Global Muslim Identity: Younger generations of Muslims, particularly in the diaspora, are redefining what it means to be Muslim in a multicultural world.

The modern world presents both obstacles and opportunities for

Islam. Whether through political engagement, academic revival, or spiritual reformation, Islam will continue to adapt, evolve, and shape global civilization in the years to come.

Conclusion: Islam in the 21st Century

Islam's interaction with modernity is dynamic and complex. While it faces challenges from political instability, ideological conflicts, and globalization, it also thrives through cultural exchange, intellectual revival, and technological advancements.

As Muslims navigate the modern world, they must balance tradition with progress, faith with reason, and identity with integration. The essence of Islam—its call for justice, knowledge, and spiritual fulfillment—remains relevant, offering guidance for both individuals and societies seeking ethical solutions in an increasingly interconnected world.

In the end, the future of Islam depends not only on religious institutions and political leaders but also on the everyday Muslim—the student, the scholar, the entrepreneur, and the activist—who seeks to live out their faith with purpose, dignity, and conviction in a world that is constantly changing.

Islam and Judaism

Shared history, theological similarities, and differences.

Islam and Judaism, two of the world's major monotheistic religions, share a deep and intertwined history that dates back to the earliest days of revelation. Both faiths trace their origins to Prophet Abraham (Ibrahim, peace be upon him) and recognize the concept of one, indivisible God (Tawhid in Islam and Shema Yisrael in Judaism). Their sacred scriptures contain overlapping narratives, their legal traditions share a commitment to divine law, and their communities have coexisted—sometimes in harmony, sometimes in tension—over centuries.

To understand the relationship between Islam and Judaism, one must explore their historical connections, theological commonalities, and doctrinal differences. While both religions have distinct spiritual frameworks, their shared principles have shaped the way they have interacted throughout history.

1. Historical Interactions Between Muslims and Jews

The historical relationship between Islam and Judaism can be divided into key phases:

A. Pre-Islamic Arabia and Jewish Communities

Before the rise of Islam, several Jewish tribes lived in the Arabian Peninsula, particularly in Medina (then called Yathrib), Khaybar, and Tayma. These Jewish communities were well-established and played significant roles in trade, scholarship, and politics. They were known for their monotheistic beliefs, adherence to the Torah, and expertise in commerce and agriculture.

When Prophet Muhammad (peace be upon him) migrated to Medina in 622 CE (Hijrah), he encountered these Jewish communities.

He established the Constitution of Medina, a social contract that recognized Jews as part of the broader community (Ummah), granting them religious freedom and civic rights. This was a significant moment in interfaith relations, demonstrating Islam's early commitment to coexistence with the People of the Book (Ahl al-Kitab).

B. The Golden Age of Islamic-Jewish Relations

During the Islamic Golden Age (8th–14th centuries), Jews flourished in Muslim-ruled lands, particularly in Al-Andalus (Islamic Spain), the Ottoman Empire, and Persia. Under Islamic rule, Jewish scholars and scientists made groundbreaking contributions in fields such as medicine, astronomy, and philosophy. Some notable Jewish figures who thrived under Islamic governance include:

Maimonides (Ibn Maymun, 1138–1204 CE): A Jewish philosopher, physician, and theologian who lived in Muslim Spain and Egypt and was heavily influenced by Islamic philosophical thought.

Saadia Gaon (882–942 CE): A Jewish scholar in Abbasid Baghdad who engaged in theological debates with Muslim scholars and wrote in Arabic.

Jewish communities in the Muslim world enjoyed a protected status under Islamic law (dhimmi status), which allowed them to practice their faith freely in exchange for paying a tax (jizya). While they were considered second-class citizens in some respects, they generally faced less persecution under Islamic rule than under Christian Europe, where Jews were often expelled or forcibly converted.

C. Conflicts and Tensions in Later Centuries

The modern period brought challenges to Islamic-Jewish relations, particularly due to European colonialism, nationalist movements, and the establishment of the state of Israel in 1948. While historically, Jews and Muslims coexisted peacefully for much of Islamic history, the 20th and 21st centuries have seen political conflicts overshadow religious commonalities.

Despite these challenges, Islamic and Jewish scholars continue to engage in interfaith dialogue, recognizing that political tensions should not erase centuries of theological and cultural exchange.

2. Theological Similarities Between Islam and Judaism

Despite their differences, Islam and Judaism share many core theological beliefs and religious practices:

A. Monotheism: Belief in One God

Both Islam and Judaism adhere to strict monotheism.

In Islam, Tawhid is the fundamental belief that God (Allah) is one, unique, and indivisible.

In Judaism, the Shema Yisrael ("Hear, O Israel, the Lord is our God, the Lord is One") is the defining statement of Jewish faith in one God.

Unlike Christianity, which introduced the concept of the Trinity, both Islam and Judaism reject any division in God's nature, emphasizing pure monotheism.

B. Divine Law: Shariah and Halakha

Both religions place significant emphasis on divine law as the guiding principle for daily life:

Shariah (Islamic law) and Halakha (Jewish law) regulate aspects of worship, dietary restrictions, marriage, business transactions, and ethical conduct.

Both traditions have religious scholars (Ulama in Islam, Rabbis in Judaism) who interpret these laws based on scripture, legal rulings, and scholarly consensus.

For example, both Islam and Judaism prohibit the consumption of pork and alcohol, practice ritual slaughter (Zabihah in Islam, Shechita in Judaism), and emphasize modesty in dress and behavior.

C. Prophets and Revelation

Islam and Judaism recognize many of the same prophets, including:

Adam (Adam)
Noah (Nuh)
Abraham (Ibrahim)
Moses (Musa)
David (Dawud)
Solomon (Sulaiman)

Islam regards Moses (Musa) as one of the greatest prophets and acknowledges that he received divine revelation (Tawrat = Torah). However, Islam teaches that over time, some aspects of the Torah were altered, and thus the final, unaltered revelation is the Qur'an.

3. Key Differences Between Islam and Judaism

Despite their many similarities, Islam and Judaism also have significant theological and doctrinal differences:

A. The Role of Jesus and Muhammad

In Islam, Jesus (Isa) is considered a prophet and the Messiah, but not divine. Islam rejects the crucifixion, believing instead that God raised Jesus to heaven.

In Judaism, Jesus is not recognized as the Messiah or a prophet and holds no central religious significance.

Most crucially, Islam regards Prophet Muhammad as the final prophet (Khatam an-Nabiyyin), while Judaism does not acknowledge him as a prophet.

B. The Concept of the Chosen People vs. the Universal Message

Judaism sees the Jewish people as God's "chosen people," with a unique covenant (Brit) with God.

Islam teaches that its message is for all of humanity, regardless of ethnicity. There is no chosen race or nation in Islam, only believers (mu'minun) and non-believers (kafirun).

C. Views on the Afterlife

Both Islam and Judaism believe in resurrection and divine judgment, but Jewish teachings on the afterlife are less detailed and vary between different schools of thought.

Islam has a more structured concept of Heaven (Jannah) and Hell (Jahannam), with vivid descriptions in the Qur'an and Hadith.

Conclusion: A Relationship of Shared Faith and Historical Complexity

Islam and Judaism share a deep theological foundation, a common ethical framework, and a long history of coexistence. While political tensions have often strained relations, their shared belief in one God, commitment to divine law, and reverence for the same prophets serve as a powerful reminder of their interconnectedness.

Throughout history, Muslim and Jewish scholars, merchants, and communities have worked together, debated theology, and enriched each other's cultures. Today, as interfaith dialogue grows, many Muslims and Jews are recognizing that their historical bonds far outweigh the divisions imposed by contemporary geopolitics.

By focusing on shared values, mutual respect, and a commitment to peace, Islam and Judaism have the potential to rebuild bridges of understanding, just as they did in the great civilizations of the past.

Islam and Christianity

The role of Jesus in Islam, theological divergences, and historical interactions.

Islam and Christianity, the world's two largest religions, share deep historical and theological connections. Both faiths originate from the Abrahamic tradition, believe in one omnipotent God, and share many of the same prophets, moral teachings, and eschatological beliefs. Yet, despite these similarities, they also have significant theological differences, particularly concerning the nature of God, the role of Jesus (Isa, peace be upon him), and salvation.

From the early interactions between Muslims and Christians in the Arabian Peninsula to the intellectual exchanges of the Islamic Golden Age, and the complex political and military encounters during the Crusades and beyond, the relationship between Islam and Christianity has fluctuated between cooperation, competition, and conflict.

This chapter explores the role of Jesus in Islam, key theological divergences, and the historical encounters between the two faiths, shedding light on how their shared past continues to shape their present and future interactions.

1. The Role of Jesus in Islam

One of the most misunderstood aspects of Islam among Christians is the Islamic perspective on Jesus (Isa, peace be upon him). While Islam does not accept the Christian belief in Jesus as the Son of God or the divine Savior, it greatly honors him as a prophet and messenger of God.

A. Jesus in the Qur'an: A Revered Messenger

Jesus is one of the most prominent figures in the Qur'an, mentioned by name more than 25 times, often with great reverence.

He is called "Isa ibn Maryam" (Jesus, son of Mary), emphasizing his miraculous birth to the Virgin Mary (Maryam), who is also highly honored in Islam.

He is referred to as Al-Masih (the Messiah), though the Islamic interpretation of this title differs from the Christian understanding.

He is described as a prophet sent by God to guide the Children of Israel (Bani Isra'il), confirming the message of earlier prophets and delivering divine wisdom.

B. The Virgin Birth and Miracles

Islam fully affirms the miraculous birth of Jesus from the Virgin Mary. The Qur'an describes how Mary conceived Jesus through the divine will of God (Surah Maryam, 19:16-21). However, unlike Christianity, Islam does not interpret this event as proof of Jesus' divinity but rather as a sign of God's power, similar to how Adam was created without parents (Surah Aal-e-Imran, 3:59).

Jesus also performed many miracles in Islamic belief, including:

Speaking as a newborn to declare his prophetic mission (Surah Maryam, 19:29-30).

Healing the blind and the leper.

Giving life to the dead by God's permission.

C. The Crucifixion: A Fundamental Difference

One of the most significant differences between Islam and Christianity is the belief regarding the crucifixion of Jesus.

The Christian faith centers on the crucifixion, death, and resurrection of Jesus as the foundation of salvation.

In contrast, the Qur'an states that Jesus was not crucified but was instead raised to heaven by God:

"And [for] their saying, 'Indeed, we have killed the Messiah, Jesus, the son of Mary, the messenger of Allah.' And they did not kill him, nor did they crucify him; but [another] was made to resemble him to them..." (Surah An-Nisa, 4:157)

Muslim scholars interpret this verse in different ways:

Some believe that Jesus was taken to heaven before the crucifixion and that another person (possibly Judas or a Roman soldier) was made to appear like him.

Others suggest that the Qur'an rejects the perceived victory of Jesus' enemies, meaning that his mission was not defeated but continued through divine intervention.

Muslims believe that Jesus will return to Earth before the Day of Judgment, where he will restore justice, defeat the false Messiah (Dajjal), and affirm the worship of the one true God.

2. Theological Divergences Between Islam and Christianity

A. The Nature of God: Tawhid vs. the Trinity

The most fundamental difference between Islam and Christianity is their understanding of God's nature.

Islam strictly upholds Tawhid (absolute monotheism), emphasizing that God is one, without partners, without a son, and beyond human attributes (Surah Ikhlas, 112:1-4).

Christianity, on the other hand, believes in the Trinity (Father, Son, and Holy Spirit), which Islam categorically rejects:

"They have certainly disbelieved who say, 'Allah is the Messiah, the son of Mary.' Say, 'Then who could prevent Allah at all if He had intended to destroy the Messiah, the son of Mary, or his mother or everyone on the earth?'" (Surah Al-Ma'idah, 5:17)

Muslims view the doctrine of the Trinity as a later theological development that deviates from the pure monotheism preached by earlier prophets, including Jesus himself.

B. Salvation and Original Sin

Christianity teaches that humans inherit original sin from Adam and Eve, and salvation is only possible through faith in Jesus' atoning sacrifice.

Islam, however, does not believe in original sin. Instead, it teaches that every human is born pure, and salvation is attained through faith in God, good deeds, and sincere repentance (Surah Az-Zumar, 39:53).

C. The Role of Religious Law

Christianity, especially in its later developments, moved away from strict legal codes, emphasizing faith over law.

Islam, like Judaism, maintains a comprehensive legal framework (Shariah) that governs worship, ethics, social interactions, and justice.

3. Historical Interactions Between Muslims and Christians

A. Early Encounters: Mutual Respect and Dialogue

One of the earliest interactions between Muslims and Christians occurred when Prophet Muhammad sent persecuted Muslims to Christian Abyssinia (modern-day Ethiopia), where the righteous Christian king, Negus, granted them protection.

B. The Islamic Golden Age: Knowledge Exchange

During the Islamic Golden Age, Muslims and Christians collaborated in philosophy, science, and medicine.

Christian scholars in the Byzantine and Syriac traditions translated Greek works into Arabic.

Muslim scientists, such as Ibn Sina (Avicenna) and Al-Farabi, influenced Christian Europe during the Renaissance.

C. The Crusades: A Period of Conflict

The Crusades (1096–1291) marked centuries of conflict between Christian Europe and the Muslim world, mainly over control of Jerusalem. However, even in war, figures like Salahuddin Ayyubi (Saladin) demonstrated chivalry and respect toward Christian foes, allowing safe passage for Christian pilgrims.

D. Modern Relations and Interfaith Efforts

Today, Islam and Christianity engage in dialogue and cooperation, especially in areas of social justice, charity, and peace-building. Initiatives like the Common Word movement and Vatican-Muslim dialogues aim to foster understanding and respect between the two faiths.

Conclusion: Two Faiths with a Shared Future

Islam and Christianity, despite their theological differences, share a common heritage of faith, ethics, and devotion to God. While past conflicts have shaped their historical relationship, today, Muslims and Christians have the opportunity to build bridges of understanding.

Through interfaith dialogue, mutual respect, and shared values, both communities can work toward a future rooted in peace, justice, and the worship of the One God.

Islam and Other Faiths

Relations with Hinduism, Buddhism, Sikhism, and interfaith dialogue.

Islam has long existed in a world of religious diversity, engaging with a variety of faiths throughout its history. While its closest theological connections are with the other Abrahamic religions—Judaism and Christianity—Islam has also interacted with Eastern traditions such as Hinduism, Buddhism, and Sikhism, particularly in regions like India, Central Asia, and Southeast Asia. These encounters have ranged from intellectual exchanges and cultural syncretism to conflict and competition, but they have also fostered moments of deep mutual influence.

At its core, Islam upholds the principle of Tawhid (oneness of God) and asserts itself as the final revelation, but it also acknowledges the presence of previous religious traditions and promotes dialogue and peaceful coexistence. The Qur'an affirms:

"Indeed, those who believe, and those who are Jews, and the Christians, and the Sabians—whoever believes in Allah and the Last Day and does righteousness—will have their reward with their Lord, and no fear will there be concerning them, nor will they grieve." (Surah Al-Baqarah, 2:62)

While theological differences between Islam and Eastern religions remain significant, history shows that Islamic civilization has often been shaped by its interactions with non-Abrahamic traditions. From Persian Zoroastrianism to Indian Hinduism and Buddhism, these exchanges have influenced Islamic art, philosophy, and cultural practices.

This chapter explores Islam's historical and theological relations with Hinduism, Buddhism, Sikhism, and the modern landscape of interfaith dialogue.

1. Islam and Hinduism: A Complex Relationship

Hinduism is one of the oldest surviving religious traditions, with sacred texts and beliefs that predate Islam by thousands of years. Unlike Islam, which is strictly monotheistic, Hinduism is polytheistic and henotheistic, with varied beliefs in deities, avatars, and cosmic principles. Despite these differences, Islam and Hinduism have a long and intricate history, particularly in India, where the two faiths have coexisted for over a millennium.

A. Islamic Views on Hinduism

Islamic scholars historically debated whether Hindus could be classified as People of the Book (Ahl al-Kitab) like Jews and Christians. While Hindus do not follow a single scripture akin to the Qur'an or Torah, some Islamic thinkers suggested that Hinduism's Vedas and Upanishads could be considered divinely inspired texts that were later altered. This view allowed for social and legal accommodations between Hindus and Muslims in regions where they lived together.

B. Islamic-Hindu Interactions in India

Islam was introduced to India in the 7th century through Arab traders, but it gained political prominence during the Delhi Sultanate (1206–1526) and the Mughal Empire (1526–1857). Under Mughal rule, figures like Emperor Akbar sought religious pluralism, promoting dialogue between Muslim scholars and Hindu sages. Akbar even founded a syncretic faith called Din-i-Ilahi, blending elements of Islam and Hinduism.

However, the relationship between Hindus and Muslims in India has also been marked by episodes of conflict, including periods of forced conversions, temple destructions, and communal tensions, particularly during the partition of India in 1947. Today, India remains home to one of the largest Muslim populations in the world, and Hindu-Muslim relations continue to evolve amid both political tensions and grassroots interfaith efforts.

2. Islam and Buddhism: Intellectual and Historical Encounters

Buddhism, founded by Siddhartha Gautama (the Buddha) in the 5th–4th century BCE, emphasizes non-theistic spiritual liberation, meditation, and ethical conduct. Unlike Islam, which is deeply theocentric, Buddhism focuses on the cessation of suffering (Dukkha) and enlightenment (Nirvana).

A. The Spread of Islam in Buddhist Regions

Islam and Buddhism first encountered each other in Central Asia, Persia, and the Indian subcontinent, particularly after the Muslim conquests of Buddhist regions such as Gandhara and Nalanda in the 7th–12th centuries. Many Buddhist monks and scholars converted to Islam or migrated to regions where Buddhism remained dominant, such as Tibet and China.

Despite initial conflicts, Islamic civilization eventually absorbed Buddhist influences in areas such as:

Sufism: Some scholars argue that Sufi practices, such as meditation and asceticism, were influenced by Buddhist monastic traditions.

Art and Architecture: Islamic architecture in regions like Afghanistan and China reflects Buddhist influences in geometric patterns, pagoda-like structures, and fresco techniques.

B. Coexistence in Southeast Asia

In regions like Indonesia, Malaysia, and Thailand, Buddhists and Muslims have coexisted for centuries, often blending cultural practices. Today, tensions exist in some areas—such as the Rohingya crisis in Myanmar, where a Muslim minority faces persecution from the Buddhist-majority government—but many efforts at interfaith peacebuilding continue.

3. Islam and Sikhism: Shared Histories and Differences

Sikhism was founded in 15th-century India by Guru Nanak (1469–1539 CE), during a time of Hindu-Muslim interactions under Mughal rule. Sikhism incorporates elements of both Islamic and Hindu traditions but stands as a distinct monotheistic faith.

A. Similarities Between Islam and Sikhism

Monotheism: Sikhs, like Muslims, believe in one, formless God (Waheguru).

Equality and Justice: Both Islam and Sikhism emphasize social justice, charity, and equality before God.

Spiritual Devotion: Islam's dhikr (remembrance of God) is similar to Sikhism's Naam Simran (continuous meditation on God's name).

B. Conflicts and Cooperation

The Mughal-Sikh relationship was complex. While some Mughal rulers persecuted Sikh leaders, Sikhism also found inspiration in Islamic teachings on devotion and ethics. Today, Muslims and Sikhs continue to engage in interfaith initiatives, particularly in South Asia and the diaspora communities in the West.

4. Interfaith Dialogue: The Islamic Perspective

Islamic teachings emphasize respect and peaceful coexistence with followers of other faiths. The Qur'an states:

"Invite to the way of your Lord with wisdom and good instruction, and argue with them in a way that is best." (Surah An-Nahl, 16:125)

Throughout history, Muslim scholars and leaders have engaged in interfaith dialogues with Hindus, Buddhists, and Sikhs, seeking common ground while maintaining their distinct religious identity.

A. Modern Interfaith Initiatives

In the contemporary world, Muslims actively participate in interfaith dialogue to promote mutual understanding. Some key initiatives include:

The Amman Message (2004): A global Islamic call for intra-Muslim unity and interfaith peace.

The Parliament of the World's Religions: An ongoing platform where Muslim scholars engage with Hindu, Buddhist, and Sikh leaders.

Muslim-Hindu Reconciliation Efforts: Efforts in India, Pakistan, and the West to address communal tensions and promote harmony.

Conclusion: A Path Toward Understanding and Peace

Islam's encounters with Hinduism, Buddhism, and Sikhism have shaped centuries of cultural exchange, intellectual discourse, and, at times, conflict. While theological differences remain, Islam emphasizes respect, dialogue, and peaceful engagement with other faiths.

In a world where religious and cultural diversity is unavoidable, mutual respect and understanding remain key to peaceful coexistence. As the Qur'an reminds:

"To you, your religion, and to me, mine." (Surah Al-Kafirun, 109:6)

Through continued interfaith dialogue and efforts toward peace, Muslims and followers of other traditions can work together to build a world rooted in justice, harmony, and respect for the Creator and His creation.

Islamic Spirituality and Worship

The concept of Ihsan (spiritual excellence) and inner purification.

Islam is not merely a system of laws, rituals, and beliefs—it is a holistic way of life that emphasizes not only outward compliance but also inner transformation. At the heart of Islamic spirituality lies the concept of Ihsan (spiritual excellence), a profound state of awareness and devotion that elevates worship from a mere obligation to an intimate connection with the Divine.

Islamic spirituality is not confined to ritual acts of worship; rather, it extends to inner purification, self-discipline, moral character, and constant awareness of God (Taqwa). This spiritual journey is deeply embedded in Islamic teachings, as reflected in the Qur'an and the sayings of Prophet Muhammad (peace be upon him).

This chapter explores the concept of Ihsan, the significance of inner purification (Tazkiyah al-Nafs), and how these elements shape the spiritual life of a believer.

1. Ihsan: The Pinnacle of Faith

The word Ihsan comes from the Arabic root h-s-n, meaning "to do good" or "to perfect something." In the Islamic context, Ihsan refers to spiritual excellence, sincerity in worship, and a deep sense of consciousness of God (Allah).

The most famous definition of Ihsan comes from the Hadith of Jibril, where the Angel Gabriel came to the Prophet Muhammad (peace be upon him) in the form of a man and asked:

"Tell me about Ihsan."

The Prophet (peace be upon him) replied:

"Ihsan is to worship Allah as if you see Him, and if you cannot see

Him, then know that He sees you." (Sahih Muslim)

This definition highlights two levels of God-consciousness:

Worshipping as if one sees God (Mushahadah) – This represents the highest level of spiritual awareness, where a believer's faith is so strong that they feel as though they are in the direct presence of Allah.

Knowing that God sees you (Muraqabah) – Even if a person does not reach the state of Mushahadah, they must remain aware that Allah is always watching. This instills sincerity and humility in their actions.

Thus, Ihsan transforms religious practice into an act of deep devotion, preventing worship from becoming mechanical and ensuring that a believer's actions are rooted in sincerity (Ikhlas).

2. Inner Purification: Tazkiyah al-Nafs

Islamic spirituality places great emphasis on purifying the soul (Tazkiyah al-Nafs). The Qur'an states:

"He has succeeded who purifies it (the soul), and he has failed who instills it with corruption." (Surah Ash-Shams, 91:9-10)

Tazkiyah refers to the process of inner purification, which involves removing negative traits such as arrogance, envy, greed, and hypocrisy and replacing them with sincerity, humility, gratitude, and trust in God.

A. The Three Stages of the Soul (Nafs)

Islamic scholars describe three stages of the soul's development:

Nafs al-Ammarah (The Commanding Soul) – This is the lowest state of the soul, which inclines toward evil, desires, and heedlessness. The Qur'an describes it as:

"Indeed, the soul is inclined to evil..." (Surah Yusuf, 12:53)

Nafs al-Lawwamah (The Self-Reproaching Soul) – This is a state where the soul becomes aware of its flaws and begins to struggle against temptation. The Qur'an acknowledges this:

"And I do swear by the self-reproaching soul..." (Surah Al-Qiyamah, 75:2)

Nafs al-Mutma'innah (The Tranquil Soul) – This is the highest level, where the soul attains peace and contentment through submission to God. Allah describes it in the Qur'an:

"O tranquil soul, return to your Lord, well-pleased and pleasing [to Him]." (Surah Al-Fajr, 89:27-28)

A true believer strives to move from the lowest state (Nafs al-Ammarah) to the highest state (Nafs al-Mutma'innah) through self-discipline, constant remembrance of God (Dhikr), and sincerity in worship.

3. Acts of Worship and Spiritual Connection

Islam provides various means of spiritual growth and purification, primarily through acts of worship. These are not just rituals, but opportunities for a deeper connection with God.

A. Salah (Prayer) – The Spiritual Lifeline

The five daily prayers are a direct link between a believer and Allah. They serve as a reminder of divine presence, an opportunity for repentance, and a source of inner peace.

The Qur'an states:

"Indeed, prayer prevents immorality and wrongdoing." (Surah Al-Ankabut, 29:45)

Praying with Khushu' (humility and focus) enhances spirituality and allows a believer to experience Ihsan in its true form—worshipping as if they see God.

B. Dhikr (Remembrance of God) – Nourishment for the Soul

The Prophet Muhammad (peace be upon him) said:

"The example of one who remembers Allah and one who does not is like that of the living and the dead." (Sahih al-Bukhari)

Frequent remembrance of God softens the heart, removes anxiety, and brings spiritual tranquility. Some common phrases include:

SubhanAllah (Glory be to God)

Alhamdulillah (All praise be to God)

Allahu Akbar (God is the Greatest)

C. Fasting (Sawm) – A Path to Inner Discipline

Fasting in Ramadan is not just about abstaining from food and drink but also about controlling desires, avoiding sins, and purifying the heart. The Prophet (peace be upon him) said:

"Fasting is a shield; so when one of you fasts, he should not engage in obscene speech or fight." (Sahih al-Bukhari)

Fasting instills self-discipline, gratitude, and a heightened awareness of God, embodying the spirit of Ihsan.

4. The Role of Sufism in Islamic Spirituality

Sufism (Tasawwuf) is often seen as the spiritual dimension of Islam, focusing on inner purification, devotion, and divine love. While it has different interpretations, mainstream Sufism aligns with Islamic teachings and seeks to achieve Ihsan through deep remembrance of God (Dhikr), ascetic practices, and moral refinement.

Famous Sufi scholars like Imam Al-Ghazali, Rumi, and Sheikh Abdul Qadir Jilani emphasized the balance between Islamic law (Shariah) and spiritual depth (Haqiqah), showing that spiritual excellence and religious practice must go hand in hand.

Conclusion: The Journey Toward Spiritual Excellence

Ihsan is the essence of Islamic spirituality, urging believers to elevate their worship, purify their hearts, and develop a profound awareness of God. It is not merely about following rules but about experiencing the presence of Allah in every moment of life.

By purifying the soul, practicing sincere worship, and cultivating moral excellence, a believer embarks on a journey toward inner peace and divine closeness. As the Qur'an reminds:

"And strive for Allah with the striving due to Him. He has chosen you and has not placed upon you in the religion any hardship..." (Surah Al-Hajj, 22:78)

Ultimately, the path to Ihsan and inner purification is a lifelong endeavor—one that requires constant self-reflection, devotion, and love for the Creator. Through this journey, a believer moves from ritual to reality, from form to essence, and from knowledge to divine experience.

Death and the Afterlife in Islam

Islamic eschatology, resurrection, and paradise/hell.

Death is an inevitable reality that all human beings must face. In Islam, death is not the end but a transition to the afterlife (Akhirah), which is central to Islamic theology. The belief in life after death shapes the moral framework of a Muslim's existence, reinforcing accountability and the purpose of human life. The Qur'an frequently reminds believers of the temporary nature of the worldly life and the eternal consequences of one's actions in the Hereafter.

Muslims believe in a linear concept of time, where life begins with creation, is followed by death, and then continues with resurrection (Qiyamah), divine judgment, and eternal life in either Paradise (Jannah) or Hell (Jahannam). This doctrine provides a moral compass, urging individuals to lead righteous lives in anticipation of divine justice.

This chapter explores Islamic teachings on death, the grave, the Day of Judgment, resurrection, and the realities of Paradise and Hell, drawing from Qur'anic verses and Hadith.

1. The Moment of Death: The Soul's Departure

Islam teaches that at the moment of death, the soul (Ruh) separates from the body, a process known as Sakarat al-Mawt (the agony of death). The Qur'an describes this moment vividly:

"Why then, when the soul reaches the throat, and you are looking on—but We are nearer to him than you, though you do not see."

(Surah Al-Waqi'ah, 56:83-85)

The Prophet Muhammad (peace be upon him) described the death of a believer and a disbeliever in different ways:

For the righteous, the soul exits gently, like water flowing from a jug, welcomed by angels of mercy.

For the wicked, the soul is extracted harshly, as if being torn from the body, met by angels of torment.

Once separated, the soul embarks on the next stage of its journey—the life of the grave (Barzakh).

2. The Life of the Grave: Barzakh

Barzakh is the intermediate realm between death and resurrection. It is described as a waiting period, where the soul remains conscious but separated from the physical world. The experience of Barzakh varies depending on one's deeds:

For the righteous:

The grave becomes spacious and illuminated.

The soul enjoys peace and visions of Paradise.

A window to Jannah is opened, giving glimpses of the promised reward.

For the wicked:

The grave becomes constricting and dark.

The soul experiences fear and torment.

A window to Jahannam is opened, showing its horrors.

The Prophet (peace be upon him) described the questioning of the grave, where two angels, Munkar and Nakir, interrogate the deceased:

Who is your Lord?

What is your religion?

Who is your Prophet?

Those who answer correctly receive comfort, while those who fail suffer punishment until the Day of Judgment.

3. The Day of Judgment: Resurrection and Accountability

Islam teaches that all human beings will be resurrected on the Day of Judgment (Yawm al-Qiyamah), a cataclysmic event that will mark the end of the world and the beginning of eternal life.

The Qur'an states:

"On the Day when the earth will be changed into another earth, and the heavens as well, and they will come forth before Allah, the One, the Supreme." (Surah Ibrahim, 14:48)

A. The Signs of the Last Day

Before the Day of Judgment, a series of major and minor signs will unfold:

Minor signs: The increase of injustice, immorality, and chaos.

Major signs: The appearance of the Mahdi, the return of Jesus, the rise of the Antichrist (Dajjal), and the sun rising from the West.

B. The Resurrection and Gathering

All people will be resurrected from their graves.

The entire human race will be gathered on an immense plain.

The records of deeds (Suhuf) will be presented, revealing every action, no matter how small.

The Qur'an describes this moment:

"And the record [of deeds] will be placed, and you will see the criminals fearful of that within it, and they will say, 'Oh, woe to us! What is this book that leaves nothing small or great except that it has enumerated it?'" (Surah Al-Kahf, 18:49)

4. The Scale of Deeds and Divine Judgment

Muslims believe in the weighing of deeds (Mizan), where good and bad actions will be measured.

Those whose good deeds outweigh their sins will be rewarded.

Those whose sins outweigh their good deeds will be

punished—unless forgiven by Allah's mercy.

The Prophet (peace be upon him) said:

"A man's feet will not move on the Day of Judgment until he is asked about his life, his wealth, his knowledge, and how he acted upon it." (Tirmidhi)

Among the greatest intercessors will be Prophet Muhammad (peace be upon him), who will plead for the salvation of his followers.

5. The Bridge of Sirat and Entry into Paradise or Hell

After judgment, people will cross the Sirat, a bridge over Hellfire (Jahannam):

The righteous will cross swiftly, reaching Paradise safely.

The sinful will struggle, some falling into Hell.

The Qur'an states:

"And there is none of you except he will come to it [Hell]. This is upon your Lord an inevitability decreed. Then We will save those who feared Allah and leave the wrongdoers within it, on their knees." (Surah Maryam, 19:71-72)

6. Paradise (Jannah) and Hell (Jahannam)

A. The Joys of Paradise

Paradise is the eternal home of bliss for the righteous. The Qur'an describes it as:

"Gardens beneath which rivers flow, wherein they abide forever." (Surah Al-Bayyinah, 98:8)

Jannah is divided into levels, with the highest being Al-Firdaws. The rewards include:

Eternal youth and peace.

Luxurious gardens, palaces, and rivers of milk, honey, and wine.

The greatest reward: Seeing Allah.

B. The Torments of Hell

Hell is a place of punishment for those who rejected faith and committed evil. The Qur'an warns:

"Indeed, Hell has been lying in wait for the transgressors, a place of return. In which they will remain for ages unending." (Surah An-Naba, 78:21-23)

Jahannam is divided into levels, with the worst reserved for hypocrites and tyrants. The torments include:

Blazing fire and scorching winds.

Boiling water and bitter fruit.

The torment of regret and despair.

Conclusion: The Ultimate Reality

Islamic eschatology serves as a powerful reminder of accountability. The concept of the afterlife motivates believers to lead righteous lives, strive for moral excellence, and seek God's forgiveness.

The Prophet Muhammad (peace be upon him) said:

"Be in this world as a stranger or a traveler." (Sahih al-Bukhari)

By reflecting on death and the afterlife, Muslims are encouraged to prioritize their spiritual journey, preparing for the eternal life that follows.

Jihad: Meaning and Misconceptions

Spiritual struggle vs. military engagement.

Few words in Islamic terminology have been as widely misinterpreted and misunderstood as jihad. In the modern era, the term has become politicized and distorted, often equated with violence and terrorism. However, in Islamic theology and law, jihad holds a far broader and more profound meaning. It is not synonymous with war; rather, it is a struggle, an exertion of effort toward a righteous goal.

In Islamic tradition, jihad encompasses both spiritual and physical dimensions, with the inner struggle for moral and spiritual refinement often considered the greater jihad (jihad al-akbar). Meanwhile, the lesser jihad (jihad al-asghar) includes military struggle only under specific conditions, such as self-defense or protection of religious freedom.

To understand jihad properly, it is essential to separate myth from reality and explore its true meaning, Quranic foundations, historical applications, and ethical constraints.

1. The Meaning of Jihad in Islam

The word jihad comes from the Arabic root j-h-d, which means "to strive, exert effort, or struggle". It is not inherently associated with warfare but rather with any effort made in pursuit of a noble cause.

The Qur'an frequently uses the term jihad in contexts that emphasize spiritual, social, and moral struggles:

"And those who strive (jāhadū) for Us—We will surely guide them to Our ways. And indeed, Allah is with the doers of good." (Surah Al-Ankabut, 29:69)

This verse clearly refers to jihad as a spiritual endeavor, where individuals struggle against their own weaknesses, desires, and sins in the pursuit of righteousness.

2. The Two Major Types of Jihad

Islamic scholars have classified jihad into two primary categories:

A. The Greater Jihad (Jihad al-Akbar) – The Spiritual Struggle

The greater jihad is the struggle of the soul against ignorance, arrogance, selfishness, and sin. It involves:

Strengthening faith (Iman) by deepening one's relationship with Allah.

Resisting personal temptations, such as greed, envy, or dishonesty.

Performing good deeds, even when it is difficult.

Standing for justice, even at personal risk.

The Prophet Muhammad (peace be upon him) emphasized this inner struggle when he returned from a battle and told his companions:

"We have returned from the lesser jihad to the greater jihad." (Al-Bayhaqi)

When asked what the greater jihad was, he replied:

"It is the struggle against one's own self."

This statement highlights that the primary battle in Islam is the one against personal flaws and weaknesses—a lifelong effort to attain virtue and spiritual excellence.

B. The Lesser Jihad (Jihad al-Asghar) – Armed Struggle in Defense

The lesser jihad refers to military struggle, but it is highly regulated by strict conditions in Islamic law (Shariah). It is not an open-ended license for violence, nor is it a means of forced conversion.

The Qur'an explicitly states:

"There is no compulsion in religion." (Surah Al-Baqarah, 2:256)

Thus, jihad is not about imposing Islam by force. Instead, it permits armed struggle only in cases of self-defense, protection of the oppressed, or the defense of religious freedom.

"Permission [to fight] has been given to those who are being fought, because they were wronged. And indeed, Allah is competent to give them victory." (Surah Al-Hajj, 22:39)

In Islamic history, jihad was always governed by ethical guidelines to prevent unnecessary harm and injustice.

3. Ethical Guidelines for Warfare in Islam

Islamic teachings strictly regulate when and how armed jihad can be conducted. Warfare in Islam is not chaotic violence but rather a disciplined and morally bound effort. The Prophet Muhammad (peace be upon him) set forth clear rules of engagement:

Do not kill civilians, women, children, or elderly people.

Do not destroy crops, trees, or livestock.

Do not attack places of worship or harm religious leaders.

Do not fight those who seek peace or surrender.

Do not commit treachery or mutilation of enemies.

These principles of warfare, derived from the Prophet's teachings, were revolutionary for their time and are still referenced in modern discussions on the ethics of war.

The Caliph Abu Bakr, the first successor to the Prophet, instructed his army before battle:

"Do not kill women, children, or old men. Do not cut down fruit-bearing trees or destroy inhabited places."

These moral guidelines distinguish Islamic jihad from unlawful violence, making it clear that Islam prohibits terrorism, vigilantism, and indiscriminate killing.

4. Misconceptions About Jihad

In today's world, jihad is often misunderstood due to misuse by extremist groups and media distortion. Let us address some common misconceptions:

Misconception 1: Jihad Means "Holy War"

The term "holy war" does not exist in Islamic scripture. Unlike the Crusades, which were explicitly religious wars, jihad in Islam is a struggle for righteousness, and warfare is only one small part of it.

Misconception 2: Jihad Encourages Terrorism

Islam strictly forbids acts of terrorism, suicide bombing, and killing innocent people. The Qur'an states:

"Whoever kills a soul—unless for justice or corruption in the land—it is as if he has killed all of humanity." (Surah Al-Ma'idah, 5:32)

Misconception 3: Jihad Promotes Forced Conversion

Islamic history provides no evidence of forced conversions on a large scale. Muslim empires ruled for centuries over Christian, Jewish, Hindu, and Zoroastrian communities, allowing them to practice their religions freely.

Misconception 4: Jihad Is an Offensive War Against Non-Muslims

Jihad is not about conquest or aggression. The Prophet Muhammad (peace be upon him) always prioritized peaceful treaties over warfare. Even in battle, Muslims were instructed never to fight those who did not attack them first.

5. Jihad in Modern Contexts

In the modern era, jihad takes newer forms, aligning with ethical and peaceful struggles:

Intellectual Jihad: Promoting truth and justice through education.

Social Jihad: Fighting poverty, injustice, and corruption.

Economic Jihad: Working honestly and ethically to support one's family and community.

Political Jihad: Standing against tyranny and oppression.

Muslim scholars today emphasize non-violent jihad, focusing on education, humanitarian work, and spiritual development.

Conclusion: The True Essence of Jihad

Jihad is not a call to violence, but a call to self-improvement, justice, and resistance against oppression. The greatest jihad is within oneself—a battle to overcome ignorance, ego, and sin.

The Prophet Muhammad (peace be upon him) summed it up best when he said:

"The best jihad is to speak a word of truth to a tyrannical ruler." (Sunan Abu Dawood)

This statement highlights that true jihad is a moral struggle, not senseless violence. By understanding and applying jihad correctly, Muslims can work toward personal growth, social justice, and global peace.

Islamic Family Law

Marriage, divorce, inheritance, and children's rights.

Islamic family law is a central pillar of Muslim society, governing matters of marriage, divorce, inheritance, and children's rights. It is deeply rooted in the Qur'an, Hadith, and the principles of Shariah, aiming to create a harmonious, just, and morally upright family structure. Unlike many secular legal systems, Islamic family law does not simply function as a set of legal codes; rather, it is designed to reflect ethical, spiritual, and communal responsibilities that uphold the dignity and welfare of every individual within the family unit.

The family is the cornerstone of Islamic civilization, and its legal framework ensures that relationships are established on principles of mutual respect, love, and responsibility. The laws surrounding family life in Islam were revealed at a time when many societies lacked formal protections for women and children, and thus, they were revolutionary in setting clear rights and obligations for all family members.

1. Marriage in Islam: A Sacred Contract

Marriage (nikah) in Islam is considered a solemn covenant (mithaq ghaliz), a bond that is both spiritual and legal. It is not merely a contract but also an act of worship, as it is a means of fulfilling religious duties, preserving moral values, and building a strong society.

A. The Purpose of Marriage

The Qur'an highlights the purpose of marriage as follows:

"And among His signs is that He created for you spouses from among yourselves so that you may find tranquility in them; and He has placed between you affection and mercy. Indeed, in that are signs for people who reflect." (Surah Ar-Rum, 30:21)

This verse captures the three key elements of a successful Islamic marriage:

Tranquility (sakinah) – A peaceful and stable companionship.

Affection (mawaddah) – Deep love and care between spouses.

Mercy (rahmah) – Mutual kindness and understanding.

B. Conditions of a Valid Marriage

For a marriage to be valid in Islam, the following conditions must be met:

Consent of both parties – Forced marriages are invalid in Islam, as the Prophet Muhammad (peace be upon him) explicitly prohibited them.

Presence of witnesses – Marriage must be conducted in a transparent manner with at least two witnesses.

Mahr (dower) – A mandatory gift from the groom to the bride, symbolizing financial security.

Public announcement – Islam discourages secret marriages, emphasizing openness and community involvement.

C. Women's Rights in Marriage

Islam significantly enhanced women's rights in marriage, granting them:

The right to choose their spouse – A woman cannot be forced into marriage against her will.

The right to financial support (nafaqah) – Husbands are required to provide for their wives.

The right to retain their identity – A woman keeps her maiden name after marriage.

The right to seek divorce (khula') – A woman can initiate divorce if the marriage becomes unbearable.

2. Divorce in Islam: A Last Resort

While Islam strongly encourages reconciliation in troubled marriages, it permits divorce as a last resort when all efforts fail. The Qur'an states:

"And if you fear dissension between them, send an arbitrator from his people and an arbitrator from her people. If they both desire reconciliation, Allah will cause it between them." (Surah An-Nisa, 4:35)

A. Types of Divorce in Islam

There are three main types of divorce in Islamic law:

Talaq (Divorce by the Husband) – A man has the right to pronounce divorce under strict conditions. However, he must allow time for reflection and avoid rash decisions.

Khula' (Divorce by the Wife) – A woman can initiate divorce by returning her mahr. This ensures financial fairness in separation.

Tafreeq (Judicial Divorce) – A judge can dissolve a marriage if a husband is abusive, negligent, or unjust.

B. The Waiting Period (Iddah)

After divorce, a woman observes a waiting period (iddah) of three menstrual cycles (or until childbirth if pregnant). This serves several purposes:

Ensuring emotional and physical well-being.

Confirming pregnancy status.

Providing a chance for reconciliation.

Islamic divorce is not a hasty or casual process; it is highly structured to protect both spouses and prevent injustice.

3. Inheritance in Islam: A Fair System

Islamic inheritance law (Faraid) is detailed in the Qur'an and ensures wealth is distributed fairly among heirs. Unlike some historical legal systems that favored male heirs exclusively, Islam introduced a fixed, just, and transparent inheritance system.

A. Qur'anic Guidelines on Inheritance

The Qur'an outlines clear shares for family members:

"Allah commands you regarding your children: for the male, a portion equal to that of two females..." (Surah An-Nisa, 4:11)

While this verse has been misunderstood, it does not signify discrimination against women. Instead, it reflects the financial responsibilities assigned to men in Islamic society—as men are obligated to provide for their families, while women retain their wealth.

B. Who Inherits in Islam?

The primary heirs in Islam include:

Spouses – Husbands and wives inherit from each other.

Children – Sons and daughters receive fixed shares.

Parents – If alive, they receive portions of the inheritance.

Siblings and extended relatives – If no direct heirs exist, inheritance extends to the wider family.

Islamic inheritance laws prevent disputes and ensure economic stability within families.

4. Children's Rights in Islam

Islamic family law places great emphasis on the rights of children, ensuring they are protected, nurtured, and given opportunities for a righteous life.

A. The Right to Life and Care

The Qur'an explicitly condemns female infanticide, a common practice in pre-Islamic Arabia:

"And when the girl [who was] buried alive is asked: For what sin was she killed?" (Surah At-Takwir, 81:8-9)

Children in Islam have the right to a loving family, proper education, and financial support.

B. The Right to a Good Name and Identity

The Prophet Muhammad (peace be upon him) instructed parents to give their children good names and raise them with dignity.

C. The Right to Education and Upbringing

The Prophet said:

"The best gift a father can give his child is good education." (Sunan Al-Tirmidhi)

Islamic teachings emphasize both religious and worldly education for boys and girls alike.

D. The Right to Inheritance and Financial Security

Children—especially orphans—are given special protection in Islamic law. The Qur'an warns against misusing an orphan's wealth:

"Do not approach the orphan's property except in the best manner until he reaches maturity." (Surah Al-An'am, 6:152)

Conclusion: The Holistic Nature of Islamic Family Law

Islamic family law is not merely a legal system—it is a comprehensive framework designed to uphold justice, compassion, and social harmony. It ensures that marriages are built on love, divorces are conducted with dignity, wealth is distributed fairly, and children are raised with rights and responsibilities.

By understanding the wisdom behind these laws, one can see how Islam places family at the heart of its civilization, ensuring balance between duty, love, and justice.

Muslim Holidays and Festivals

Eid al-Fitr, Eid al-Adha, and other significant celebrations.

Islamic holidays and festivals are deeply spiritual occasions that connect Muslims to their faith, history, and community. These celebrations mark significant religious events, reflect Islamic values, and serve as opportunities for gratitude, generosity, and worship. Unlike secular holidays, Islamic celebrations are deeply intertwined with acts of devotion, such as prayer, charity, and remembrance of Allah.

The two most important Islamic festivals—Eid al-Fitr and Eid al-Adha—are often referred to as the two great Eids, as they were designated by Prophet Muhammad (peace be upon him) himself. In addition to these, other significant occasions, such as Islamic New Year, Mawlid al-Nabi (the Prophet's birthday), and Ashura, are observed by different Muslim communities worldwide, though some are debated in terms of religious legitimacy.

1. Eid al-Fitr: The Festival of Breaking the Fast

Eid al-Fitr, meaning "Festival of Breaking the Fast," is celebrated at the end of Ramadan, the sacred month of fasting. It is one of the most joyous days in Islam, as it marks not only the completion of a month of devotion but also an opportunity for charity, communal prayer, and gratitude.

A. The Significance of Eid al-Fitr

The Prophet Muhammad (peace be upon him) emphasized the importance of Eid al-Fitr, stating:

"Every nation has its festival, and this is your festival." (Sahih Bukhari)

Eid al-Fitr is a time of celebration, but also of spiritual renewal, where Muslims reflect on the discipline, patience, and self-restraint practiced during Ramadan.

B. Rituals and Traditions

The celebration of Eid al-Fitr follows specific religious and cultural traditions, including:

Sighting of the Moon – Eid is declared upon the sighting of the new moon, marking the first day of Shawwal, the month after Ramadan.

Giving Zakat al-Fitr – Before the Eid prayer, every Muslim is required to give charity (Zakat al-Fitr) to the poor. This ensures that everyone can partake in the celebration, even those in financial hardship.

Eid Prayer (Salat al-Eid) – Muslims gather in mosques or open fields for a special congregational prayer, usually early in the morning.

Festive Meals and Gatherings – After the prayer, families and friends come together to share meals, exchange gifts, and visit loved ones.

Wearing New Clothes – It is a tradition to wear new or clean, beautiful clothes as a sign of gratitude to Allah.

Eid al-Fitr is not just about feasting and joy; it is also a day of forgiveness, family unity, and spiritual reflection.

2. Eid al-Adha: The Festival of Sacrifice

Eid al-Adha, or "The Festival of Sacrifice," is the second and most significant of the two major Islamic festivals. It coincides with the Hajj pilgrimage and commemorates the willingness of Prophet Ibrahim (Abraham) to sacrifice his son, Ismail (Ishmael), in obedience to Allah's command.

A. The Story Behind Eid al-Adha

According to Islamic tradition, Prophet Ibrahim dreamed that Allah commanded him to sacrifice his son as a test of faith. As he prepared to carry out the sacrifice, Allah intervened and provided a ram to be sacrificed instead, rewarding Ibrahim for his unwavering submission.

This event is central to Islamic faith, as it symbolizes total devotion to Allah, faith in divine wisdom, and the importance of obedience to God's will. The Qur'an mentions:

"We ransomed him with a mighty sacrifice." (Surah As-Saffat, 37:107)

B. Rituals and Traditions

Eid Prayer – As with Eid al-Fitr, Muslims gather for a special Eid prayer in mosques or open spaces.

Qurbani (Sacrificial Offering) – Muslims who can afford to do so perform the ritual slaughter of an animal (usually a sheep, goat, cow, or camel).

The meat is divided into three parts:

One-third for the family.

One-third for relatives and friends.

One-third for the poor and needy.

Distributing Charity – As Eid al-Adha emphasizes compassion and generosity, Muslims give money, food, and gifts to the less fortunate.

Hajj Pilgrimage – Eid al-Adha falls on the 10th day of Dhu al-Hijjah, during the final rites of Hajj, Islam's sacred pilgrimage to Mecca.

Eid al-Adha is a festival of faith, gratitude, and community service, reminding Muslims of the importance of sacrifice and charity.

3. Other Significant Islamic Celebrations

A. Islamic New Year (Hijri New Year)

The Islamic New Year, also called Hijri New Year, marks the beginning of the lunar calendar. It is a time of reflection rather than festivity, as it commemorates the Hijrah (migration) of Prophet Muhammad and his followers from Mecca to Medina in 622 CE.

B. Mawlid al-Nabi: The Prophet's Birthday

Mawlid al-Nabi is observed on the 12th of Rabi' al-Awwal, marking the birth of Prophet Muhammad.

In many Muslim-majority countries, public gatherings, recitations of the Prophet's life (Seerah), and acts of charity take place.

However, some scholars debate its religious validity, arguing that it was not observed by the Prophet's companions.

C. Ashura: A Day of Reflection and Remembrance

Ashura falls on the 10th of Muharram and is observed differently among Sunni and Shi'a Muslims:

For Sunnis, it is a day of fasting in remembrance of Prophet Musa (Moses) and the Israelites' rescue from Pharaoh.

For Shi'a Muslims, it is a day of mourning, commemorating the martyrdom of Imam Husayn, the grandson of Prophet Muhammad, at the Battle of Karbala in 680 CE.

D. Laylat al-Qadr: The Night of Power

Laylat al-Qadr, occurring in the last ten nights of Ramadan, is the holiest night in Islam, believed to be the night when the first verses of the Qur'an were revealed. Worship on this night is regarded as more powerful than a thousand months.

E. Laylat al-Miraj: The Night Journey

Laylat al-Miraj commemorates the Prophet Muhammad's miraculous night journey (Isra and Miraj) from Mecca to Jerusalem and his ascension to the heavens.

4. The Social and Spiritual Importance of Islamic Festivals

Islamic festivals are not just cultural events; they are spiritual milestones that bring communities together and reinforce core Islamic values such as:

Gratitude to Allah – Acknowledging divine blessings through worship and charity.

Generosity and Giving – Sharing wealth and food with the less fortunate.

Family and Community Bonding – Strengthening social ties

through gatherings and celebrations.

Spiritual Reflection – Taking time to reconnect with faith and re-evaluate one's actions.

Islamic holidays ensure that faith remains an active part of daily life, integrating worship with joy, community, and social responsibility.

Conclusion

Islamic holidays and festivals are not just moments of celebration but are deeply rooted in faith, history, and worship. Eid al-Fitr and Eid al-Adha, the two great festivals, remind Muslims of self-discipline, charity, sacrifice, and devotion to Allah. Other significant occasions offer opportunities for reflection, remembrance, and community service.

Through these celebrations, Islam fosters a sense of belonging, gratitude, and commitment to righteousness, ensuring that faith is not just believed but lived and practiced.

The Role of the Mosque in Muslim Life

Religious, social, and educational functions of mosques in Islamic society.

The mosque (masjid) holds a central position in the life of a Muslim. It is more than just a place of prayer; it is a community hub, an educational institution, and a center for social welfare. From the time of the Prophet Muhammad (peace be upon him) until today, mosques have served as the heart of Muslim society, shaping religious identity, fostering unity, and providing a sanctuary for both spiritual and communal growth.

1. The Historical Significance of the Mosque

The first mosque in Islam was the Quba Mosque, built upon Prophet Muhammad's arrival in Medina. Shortly thereafter, the Prophet's Mosque (Masjid al-Nabawi) was established, becoming the spiritual and administrative center of the Muslim community. Unlike modern-day places of worship that focus primarily on religious rituals, the Prophet's Mosque functioned as a meeting place, a court of justice, an educational center, and even a shelter for the poor.

During Islamic history, as Muslim civilizations expanded, grand mosques were constructed across the world, serving as intellectual and spiritual landmarks. The Umayyad Mosque in Damascus, the Al-Aqsa Mosque in Jerusalem, and the Great Mosque of Córdoba in Spain are prime examples of how mosques were not only places of worship but also symbols of Islamic knowledge, architecture, and governance.

2. The Religious Function of Mosques

At its core, the mosque is the house of Allah, and its primary role is to facilitate worship, devotion, and connection with the Divine.

A. The Daily and Weekly Prayers

Muslims are required to perform five daily prayers (Salah), and while these can be performed anywhere, praying in congregation at the mosque is highly recommended and spiritually rewarding. The Prophet Muhammad said:

"The prayer in congregation is twenty-seven times superior to the prayer offered by a person alone." (Sahih Bukhari)

On Fridays, the mosque plays a particularly central role in Muslim life, as it hosts the Jumu'ah (Friday) prayer. This weekly congregational prayer is mandatory for adult men, and it includes a sermon (khutbah) that addresses current religious, social, and moral topics.

B. Ramadan and Special Night Prayers

During the month of Ramadan, mosques become centers of spiritual rejuvenation. Muslims gather for Taraweeh prayers, long recitations of the Qur'an performed at night, and many also engage in Itikaf, a spiritual retreat where individuals stay in the mosque for the last ten days of Ramadan to focus entirely on worship.

C. Eid Prayers and Celebrations

On the occasions of Eid al-Fitr and Eid al-Adha, mosques serve as gathering places for the entire Muslim community. Large congregational prayers are held, often in open spaces or large mosques, where Muslims come together to pray, celebrate, and reinforce social bonds.

3. The Social and Community Role of Mosques

Mosques are not exclusive to religious worship—they also serve as social centers, fostering unity, brotherhood, and social responsibility within the Muslim community.

A. A Place of Unity and Equality

One of the most profound aspects of mosques is that they remove barriers of class, race, and nationality. Every Muslim, regardless of wealth or status, stands shoulder to shoulder in prayer, emphasizing the Islamic principle of universal brotherhood.

The Prophet Muhammad highlighted this spirit of equality by welcoming all Muslims, including the poor, freed slaves, and strangers, into the mosque.

B. Support for the Needy and Charity

Mosques have traditionally played an active role in social welfare by providing:

Food for the poor through community kitchens.

Financial aid (Zakat and Sadaqah) to those in need.

Funeral services for those without family support.

In many Muslim societies, mosques function as centers of charitable efforts, ensuring that no one in the community is left without help.

C. Conflict Resolution and Community Discussions

Historically, mosques have also served as councils for dispute resolution, where community leaders, scholars, and elders mediate conflicts and offer guidance based on Islamic teachings.

Many mosques continue this tradition by offering counseling services for families, youth mentorship, and legal aid for those in distress.

4. The Educational Role of Mosques

A. The First Schools of Islam

From the earliest days of Islam, mosques were centers of knowledge. The Prophet Muhammad himself taught his companions in the mosque, and this practice continued throughout Islamic history. The first madrasahs (Islamic schools) were established within mosque courtyards, where students studied Qur'an, Hadith, Arabic, and Islamic jurisprudence (Fiqh).

B. Qur'anic and Religious Studies

Even today, mosques provide education to children and adults, teaching them:

Qur'an memorization (Hifz) and recitation (Tajweed).

The teachings of Prophet Muhammad (Hadith).

Islamic ethics and moral values.

Many famous Islamic scholars, such as Imam Abu Hanifa, Imam Malik, and Imam Al-Ghazali, began their studies in mosques, highlighting their historical significance as places of intellectual and spiritual growth.

C. Modern Educational Programs

Contemporary mosques also offer a range of educational initiatives, including:

Lectures and seminars on faith, science, and personal development.

Workshops on parenting, marriage, and financial literacy.

Interfaith dialogues to foster understanding between Muslims and people of other faiths.

5. The Mosque as a Symbol of Islamic Architecture

Mosques are not only places of worship and community service but also masterpieces of Islamic architecture, reflecting beauty, spirituality, and divine inspiration.

A. The Aesthetic and Spiritual Elements

Domes and Minarets – Represent the vastness of the heavens and the call to prayer.

Mihrab (Prayer Niche) – Indicates the Qibla (direction of Mecca) and is often adorned with intricate designs.

Calligraphy and Geometric Art – Symbolizes the divine harmony of Islamic teachings.

B. Famous Mosques Around the World

Masjid al-Haram in Mecca – The holiest mosque in Islam, housing the Kaaba.

Al-Masjid an-Nabawi in Medina – The Prophet's Mosque, second in importance.

Al-Aqsa Mosque in Jerusalem – Holds historical and spiritual significance in Islam.

The Blue Mosque in Turkey – A blend of Ottoman elegance and Islamic tradition.

6. The Contemporary Role of Mosques

In modern times, mosques continue to evolve to meet the needs of Muslim communities, acting as centers for:

Interfaith engagement – Encouraging dialogue with other religious groups.

Youth activities – Providing safe spaces for young Muslims.

Humanitarian aid – Offering emergency relief during crises.

However, challenges such as political scrutiny, Islamophobia, and urban development have affected mosques in some parts of the world. Despite this, they remain the heart of Islamic life, preserving faith, fostering unity, and serving as a beacon of knowledge and social responsibility.

Conclusion

The mosque is far more than a building for prayer—it is the foundation of Muslim spiritual, social, and intellectual life. It brings people together, promotes faith and learning, and plays a crucial role in uplifting society. From the time of Prophet Muhammad until today, mosques have stood as symbols of faith, unity, and service, embodying the very essence of Islam.

Islam and Modern Challenges

Feminism, human rights, secularism, and global geopolitics.

The modern world presents a series of profound challenges to religious traditions, and Islam is no exception. As a faith that has historically shaped civilizations, governed societies, and provided a comprehensive ethical framework, Islam finds itself at the intersection of contemporary debates about feminism, human rights, secularism, and global geopolitics. The rapid pace of globalization, technological advancements, and shifts in political ideologies have raised both opportunities and conflicts for Muslims seeking to reconcile their faith with the demands of the modern era.

1. Feminism and Women's Rights in Islam

One of the most contentious and widely debated topics regarding Islam is its stance on women's rights and gender equality. The modern feminist movement, which advocates for equal rights, opportunities, and freedoms for women, has at times clashed with traditional interpretations of Islamic gender roles. However, the historical and theological reality of Islam's approach to women is far more nuanced than often portrayed.

A. The Rights of Women in Islam

Islam was revolutionary for women's rights in 7th-century Arabia. Before Islam, Arab women had little to no legal status, and practices such as female infanticide were common. The Qur'an explicitly condemned such practices and introduced inheritance rights, marriage contracts, financial independence, and protection from exploitation for women.

The Prophet Muhammad (peace be upon him) also elevated the

status of women, declaring that "The best among you are those who are best to their wives" (Tirmidhi). Women such as Khadijah (his wife), Aisha (his wife and a prominent scholar), and Fatima (his daughter) played crucial roles in early Islamic society.

B. The Modern Debate: Feminism vs. Traditionalism

While Islam granted rights to women centuries ago, cultural interpretations and patriarchal customs have often influenced how these rights are applied. Many Muslim-majority societies still struggle with issues such as education for women, political representation, and legal rights in matters of divorce and inheritance.

Modern Islamic feminists argue that many gender inequalities in Muslim societies stem from cultural influences rather than Islam itself. Figures like Fatima Mernissi and Amina Wadud have advocated for reinterpretations of Islamic texts to promote gender equality while maintaining Islamic principles. On the other hand, traditionalists argue that Islamic gender roles—where men and women have complementary but different responsibilities—are divinely ordained and should be preserved.

One of the central questions in this debate is the issue of hijab and modesty. Some view it as a symbol of female oppression, while others see it as an act of religious empowerment and autonomy. In countries like France, laws banning the hijab in public spaces have sparked outcries over religious freedom, highlighting the broader tension between Islam and Western secular values.

2. Islam and Human Rights

The discussion of human rights in Islam is often framed around the universality of modern human rights frameworks (such as the United Nations' Universal Declaration of Human Rights) and the principles of Islamic law (Shariah). While there are overlapping values, such as justice, dignity, and freedom, conflicts arise in areas such as freedom of religion, apostasy laws, LGBTQ+ rights, and freedom of speech.

A. The Concept of Rights in Islam

Islamic teachings emphasize a balanced approach to rights and responsibilities. The Qur'an declares that "We have honored the children of Adam" (Qur'an 17:70), affirming the inherent dignity of all human beings. However, Islamic law does not view rights as absolute personal freedoms but rather as a trust from God that must be exercised within moral and ethical boundaries.

For example:

Freedom of religion is upheld in Surah Al-Baqarah (2:256): "There is no compulsion in religion". However, some traditional interpretations maintain punishments for apostasy, which contradict modern understandings of religious freedom.

Justice and fairness are central in Islam, with the Qur'an commanding believers to "stand out firmly for justice, even against your own selves" (Qur'an 4:135). However, certain applications of blasphemy laws and censorship have raised concerns about freedom of expression.

B. The Controversy Over LGBTQ+ Rights

One of the most contentious debates in modern Islam concerns LGBTQ+ rights. Islamic teachings traditionally prohibit same-sex relationships, viewing them as incompatible with divine law. However, modern human rights frameworks emphasize inclusivity and non-discrimination, leading to tensions between Islamic ethics and contemporary sexual identity movements.

Some progressive Muslim scholars argue for a reinterpretation of Islamic texts, focusing on the principles of compassion, privacy, and personal morality, while others insist that Islamic sexual ethics must remain unchanged. The debate reflects the broader challenge of negotiating faith-based morality in a rapidly changing world.

3. Secularism and the Role of Religion in Society

Secularism—the separation of religion from political and public life—poses one of the most significant challenges to Islam in the modern world. Many Muslim-majority countries are wrestling with questions of governance:

Should Islamic law (Shariah) be part of the legal system?

Can democracy and Islam coexist?

How does Islam respond to the rise of atheism and religious skepticism?

A. The Islamic Perspective on Secularism

Unlike Christianity, which underwent a separation of church and state, Islam traditionally views religion and governance as intertwined. Classical Islamic civilization was built upon a fusion of spiritual and political authority, with rulers (caliphs) expected to govern by Islamic principles.

However, colonialism, globalization, and Western influence have introduced secular governance models in Muslim countries, leading to deep ideological divides. Nations like Turkey and Tunisia have embraced secular policies, while others, such as Iran and Saudi Arabia, maintain strict Islamic governance. The question remains: Can a middle ground be found?

4. Islam in Global Geopolitics

The role of Islam in international politics has never been more significant. Muslim nations are key players in global conflicts, economic struggles, and diplomatic negotiations. The perception of Islam in Western politics, media, and security policies has shaped international relations in ways that continue to fuel misunderstandings and tensions.

A. The Post-9/11 Era and Islamophobia

Since the 9/11 attacks, Islam has been frequently associated with terrorism and extremism, leading to a rise in Islamophobia in the West.

Policies such as the "War on Terror," the invasion of Iraq, and increased surveillance of Muslim communities have led many Muslims to feel alienated and misrepresented.

At the same time, extremist groups such as ISIS and Al-Qaeda have distorted Islamic teachings, fueling global suspicion. This has placed Muslim leaders in a difficult position—on the one hand, condemning terrorism, and on the other, defending Islam from negative stereotypes.

B. Muslim Nations and the Global Order

Muslim-majority countries are actively shaping global politics:

Saudi Arabia and Iran are engaged in regional power struggles, influencing conflicts in Yemen, Syria, and Lebanon.

China's treatment of Uyghur Muslims has sparked global human rights concerns.

Muslim minorities in Europe face challenges related to integration, discrimination, and identity preservation.

Islam remains a powerful force in shaping the world, not just spiritually but politically and socially.

Conclusion

Islam's interaction with modern challenges is a complex and evolving process. From feminism and human rights to secularism and global politics, Muslims today are navigating a rapidly changing world while holding onto their faith. The challenge is not whether Islam can adapt, but how it can do so while staying true to its core principles. The future of Islam in the modern world depends on engagement, intellectual rigor, and the ability to balance tradition with progress.

Further Reading

For readers seeking a deeper understanding of Islam, the following books and scholarly works cover a wide range of topics, from theology and history to law, philosophy, and mysticism. These works will serve as an excellent foundation for further study.

1. General Introductions to Islam

Karen Armstrong – Islam: A Short History

A concise yet comprehensive overview of Islam's origins, its expansion, and its role in world history.

Seyyed Hossein Nasr – Islam: Religion, History, and Civilization

A well-written introduction to Islamic teachings, culture, and contributions to civilization.

John L. Esposito – Islam: The Straight Path

A balanced introduction to the faith, covering beliefs, practices, and modern issues.

Fazlur Rahman – Islam

An insightful analysis of Islamic thought and its development through history.

Malise Ruthven – Islam: A Very Short Introduction

A brief yet informative guide to Islamic beliefs and history.

2. The Life of Prophet Muhammad

Martin Lings – Muhammad: His Life Based on the Earliest Sources

A beautifully written biography based on classical Islamic sources.

Tariq Ramadan – In the Footsteps of the Prophet: Lessons from the Life of Muhammad

A reflection on how the Prophet's life serves as a moral and ethical guide.

Adil Salahi – Muhammad: Man and Prophet

A detailed and accessible biography of Prophet Muhammad.

Ibn Ishaq – The Life of Muhammad (translated by A. Guillaume as The Life of Muhammad: A Translation of Ibn Ishaq's Sirat Rasul Allah)

The earliest known biography of the Prophet, based on oral traditions.

3. The Qur'an: Text, Interpretation, and Studies

M.A.S. Abdel Haleem – The Qur'an: A New Translation

A modern and accessible English translation of the Qur'an.

Toshihiko Izutsu – Ethico-Religious Concepts in the Qur'an

A deep linguistic and philosophical study of Qur'anic concepts.

Neal Robinson – Discovering the Qur'an: A Contemporary Approach to a Veiled Text

An academic study of the Qur'an's structure and themes.

Muhammad Abdel Haleem – Understanding the Qur'an: Themes and Style

A detailed analysis of Qur'anic themes and literary style.

Fazlur Rahman – Major Themes of the Qur'an

A thematic exploration of the Qur'anic worldview.

4. Hadith and Sunnah

Jonathan A.C. Brown – Hadith: Muhammad's Legacy in the Medieval and Modern World

A clear and scholarly introduction to the science of Hadith.

Muhammad Mustafa al-A'zami – Studies in Early Hadith Literature

An academic analysis of Hadith transmission and authentication.

Imam Nawawi – Riyadh as-Salihin (Gardens of the Righteous)

A compilation of key Prophetic traditions on ethics and spirituality.

Sahih al-Bukhari & Sahih Muslim (translated versions available)

The most authentic collections of Hadith in Sunni Islam.

5. Islamic Law (Shariah) and Jurisprudence (Fiqh)

Wael Hallaq – An Introduction to Islamic Law

A modern and well-structured introduction to the foundations of Shariah.

Noel J. Coulson – A History of Islamic Law

An overview of the historical development of Islamic legal traditions.

Mohammad Hashim Kamali – Principles of Islamic Jurisprudence

A detailed study of the methodology of Islamic jurisprudence.

Knut S. Vikør – Between God and the Sultan: A History of Islamic Law

Examines the development of Islamic law from classical times to the modern world.

6. Islamic Theology and Philosophy

Oliver Leaman – An Introduction to Classical Islamic Philosophy

A clear and structured introduction to Islamic philosophy.

Majid Fakhry – A History of Islamic Philosophy

A comprehensive study of Islamic philosophical thought.

Al-Ghazali – The Incoherence of the Philosophers

A key theological critique of classical philosophy by one of Islam's most influential scholars.

Ibn Rushd (Averroes) – The Incoherence of the Incoherence

A rebuttal of Al-Ghazali's arguments, defending Aristotelian philosophy in Islam.

7. Islamic Mysticism (Sufism)

William Chittick – Sufism: A Beginner's Guide

A short but insightful introduction to Sufi thought and practices.

Idries Shah – The Sufis

A classic work introducing Sufism to the Western audience.

Rumi – The Essential Rumi (translated by Coleman Barks)

A collection of poetry and wisdom from the famous Sufi mystic.

Al-Ghazali – The Revival of the Religious Sciences

A major work on Islamic spirituality and ethics.

8. Islam and Science

Seyyed Hossein Nasr – Science and Civilization in Islam

Explores the scientific contributions of the Islamic world.

George Saliba – Islamic Science and the Making of the European Renaissance

Examines how Islamic scientific thought influenced the West.

Ahmad Dallal – Islam, Science, and the Challenge of History

Analyzes the historical relationship between Islam and science.

9. Women and Gender in Islam

Fatima Mernissi – The Veil and the Male Elite: A Feminist Interpretation of Women's Rights in Islam

A critical analysis of women's roles in Islamic societies.

Leila Ahmed – Women and Gender in Islam

A historical study of the evolution of gender roles in Muslim societies.

Asma Barlas – "Believing Women" in Islam: Unreading Patriarchal Interpretations of the Qur'an

A feminist approach to Qur'anic exegesis.

10. Islam and Modernity

Tariq Ramadan – Western Muslims and the Future of Islam

Discusses the challenges of being Muslim in the modern world.

Wael Hallaq – The Impossible State: Islam, Politics, and Modernity's Moral Predicament

A deep analysis of the clash between Islamic governance and

modern nation-states.

John L. Esposito – The Future of Islam

Explores the contemporary challenges facing the Muslim world.

Epilogue

The Ever-Unfolding Story of Islam

Islam is not just a chapter in the history of the world—it is an ongoing story, woven into the fabric of civilizations, cultures, and the everyday lives of over a billion people. It is a faith that has stood the test of time, endured trials and triumphs, and continues to shape the moral, spiritual, and intellectual landscapes of the world.

From the deserts of Arabia to the bustling metropolises of the modern era, Islam has been a force of transformation. It has built empires and inspired revolutions, fostered scientific inquiry and artistic brilliance, and provided spiritual guidance to countless souls seeking purpose and meaning. It is a tradition both deeply rooted in the past and dynamically engaged with the present, constantly evolving yet firmly anchored in its foundational principles.

As we bring this book to a close, it is crucial to remember that understanding Islam is not a static endeavor. No single volume can capture the full depth of its theology, jurisprudence, history, and cultural expressions. Islam is a vast ocean of wisdom, and those who seek to grasp it must be willing to continue their journey beyond these pages.

The modern world presents new challenges and opportunities for Islam and Muslims. Questions about faith in a secular age, the reconciliation of tradition with modernity, the role of Islamic values in governance, and the evolving landscape of interfaith dialogue remain as pertinent today as ever. Islam is not immune to the complexities of globalization, technology, and shifting ideologies. Yet, at its core, it offers enduring guidance—rooted in divine revelation, reasoned scholarship, and an unwavering call to justice, mercy, and righteousness.

To the reader who has journeyed through these pages, you now carry with you a deeper understanding of Islam—not just as a religion, but as a civilization, a worldview, and a living tradition. Whether you are a Muslim seeking a renewed connection with your faith or someone from outside the tradition striving for knowledge and bridge-building, this is only the beginning.

The story of Islam is still being written. Its future is shaped not only by scholars and leaders but by the ordinary believers, the seekers, the questioners, and those willing to engage with its rich legacy. It is our hope that this book has provided you with the tools to see Islam with clarity, to appreciate its nuances, and to recognize its place in the broader human experience.

As the Qur'an reminds us:

"And say: My Lord, increase me in knowledge." (Surah Ta-Ha 20:114)

May this be the start of your journey, not the end. Seek knowledge. Ask questions. And most importantly, never stop exploring the vast and wondrous world of Islam.

THE END

Join The SUMIT Community

The journey of understanding doesn't end with a single book—it's a lifelong pursuit. **SUMIT** was designed to bring clarity to the vast worlds of business, psychology, philosophy, history, religion, and beyond. Each book distills the essence of profound ideas, influential figures, and transformative concepts, making them accessible and actionable for learners like you.

But why stop at one book? **Join the SUMIT Community** and become part of a vibrant network of curious minds dedicated to exploring and mastering the greatest ideas across disciplines.

Dive Deeper into your favorite subjects

Stay Inspired with insights from a growing library of expertly summarized knowledge

Connect with a community of learners who value growth and understanding as much as you do

Scan the QR Code Below to Join Us Today!

Together, we can continue to explore, learn, and create a legacy of knowledge that shapes our lives and the world around us. Don't just read about ideas—live them with the SUMIT Community.

(It's free, and you can unsubscribe anytime.)

Religion Summit Collection

Embark on an enlightening journey across the beliefs that shape our world. The Religion Summit Collection is more than just a series of books – it's a personal voyage of discovery through the wisdom of ages. Each volume invites you to a "summit" of ideas where Eastern philosophies meet Western traditions, ancient teachings encounter modern questions, and curiosity sparks personal growth at every turn.

Join the countless readers who view the Religion Summit Collection as a must-have resource for expanding their horizons. If you long to connect the dots between faiths or seek wisdom to navigate your own life challenges, this series is your companion. Open your mind and heart to a summit of spiritual knowledge – and prepare to see the world's religions in a whole new light.

***101 Religion Ideas* - Explore Diverse Traditions, Deepen Your Perspective, and Enrich Your Spiritual Life**

What if one book could open your mind to 101 profound insights from the world's great religions? 101 Religion Ideas is your gateway to understanding how centuries-old wisdom can empower and inspire your modern life. Unlock the wisdom of the world's religions – dive into 101 Religion Ideas today and embark on a transformative spiritual adventure.

CHRISTIANITY Summarized

A Complete Guide to the History, Beliefs, and Practices of the Christian Faith

For over two thousand years, Christianity has shaped civilizations, inspired revolutions, and transformed countless lives. But what is Christianity at its core? What do its followers truly believe? How did it evolve from a small group of disciples to the largest faith in the world?

ISLAM Summarized

A Concise Guide to Islamic Beliefs, History, Law, and Spirituality – Understanding Islam, the Qur'an, Shariah, Sufism, and Muslim Traditions

For over 1,400 years, Islam has shaped civilizations, inspired profound spiritual traditions, and influenced the course of world history. Yet, for many, it remains misunderstood—overshadowed by stereotypes and misconceptions.

BUDDHISM Summarized

A Complete Guide to Buddhist Philosophy, Teachings, and Meditation—From Theravāda to Zen and Tibetan Buddhism

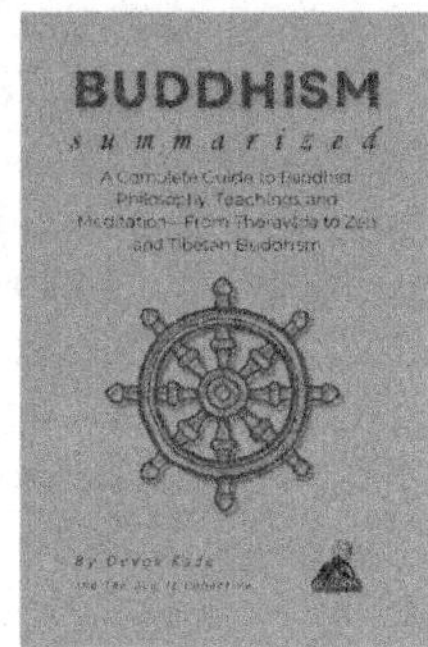

For over 2,500 years, Buddhism has transformed the lives of millions, offering a path to inner peace, clarity, and awakening. But with its vast traditions, complex philosophies, and deep meditative practices, where does one begin? Are you ready to begin your journey?

HINDUISM Summarized

A Complete Guide to Hindu Philosophy, Scriptures, Gods, Rituals, and Spiritual Wisdom

Step into the vast, awe-inspiring world of Hinduism—a tradition that has shaped the spiritual consciousness of billions for over 5,000 years. This book is your gateway to understanding the profound wisdom, sacred rituals, divine deities, and timeless philosophies that define this extraordinary faith.

JUDAISM Summarized

Everything You Need to Know About Jewish Faith, Culture, and Tradition in One Essential Book

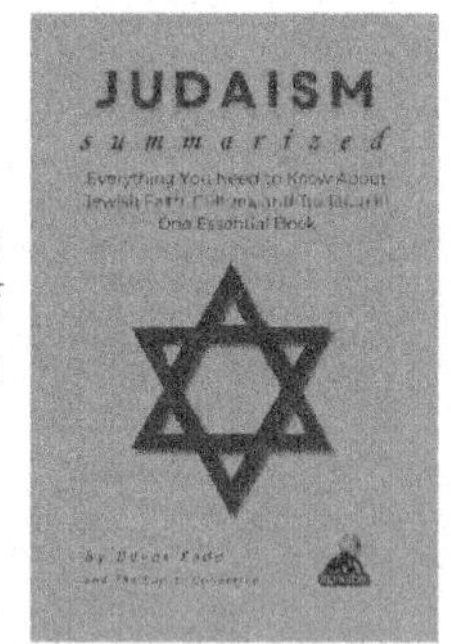

What does it truly mean to be Jewish? How has Judaism survived and thrived through centuries of exile, persecution, and renewal? Why do Jewish traditions, laws, and beliefs continue to shape the modern world? Understand Judaism. Appreciate its beauty. Engage with its future. Are you ready to discover the soul of a people?

NEW AGE & ESOTERICISM Summarized

A Complete Guide to Mysticism, Spiritual Awakening, Hidden Knowledge & Ancient Wisdom for Modern Seekers

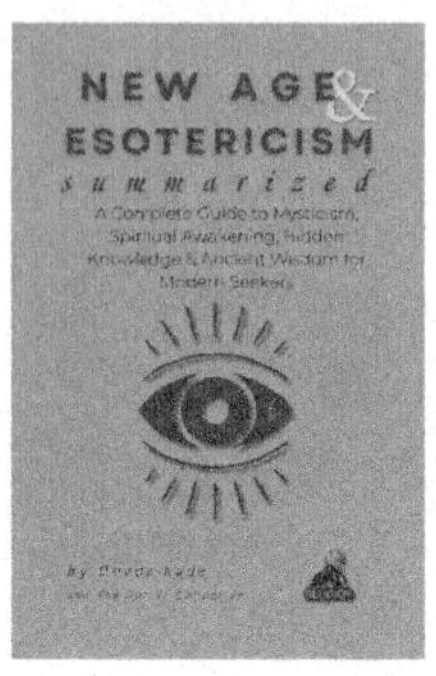

Are you ready to uncover the secrets of the cosmos, awaken your inner power, and transform your spiritual destiny? New Age & Esotericism Summarized is your ultimate guide to the mystical realms of hidden knowledge, ancient wisdom, and modern spiritual evolution.

TAOISM Summarized

Taoist Philosophy, Spirituality, and Practice for Inner Peace, Balance, and Enlightenment

For centuries, Taoism has remained an enigmatic and profound philosophy, whispering its wisdom through the Dao De Jing, the paradoxes of Zhuangzi, and the graceful movements of Tai Chi. But what if you could grasp its essence in one compelling, immersive volume? Walk the path. Embrace the flow. Live in harmony with the Tao.

COMPARATIVE RELIGION Summarized

World Religions, Beliefs, and Spiritual Traditions – Exploring Sacred Texts, Practices, and Theories Across Faiths

Religion shapes civilizations, ignites wars, heals wounds, and inspires revolutions. It weaves itself into the fabric of our existence, influencing how we love, how we fear, and how we understand the unknown. But what happens when we step back and examine it all—side by side? This is the book you've been waiting for.

MYTH & FOLK RELIGIONS Summarized

Exploring Legends, Myths, and Sacred Traditions Across Cultures – From Creation Myths to Shamanism, Folklore, and Urban Legends

Myths are more than ancient tales—they are the pulse of civilizations, the echoes of forgotten gods, and the whispers of ancestors shaping our world. From the trickster gods who defy order to the heroic figures who battle darkness, myths illuminate the human experience in ways both mystical and profound.

WICCA & PAGANISM Summarized

Exploring Witchcraft, Magic, Rituals, Spells, Wiccan Beliefs, and Ancient Pagan Traditions

Unlock the Mysteries of Wicca and Paganism—A Journey into Ancient Wisdom, Magic, and Spiritual Awakening! No fluff. No gimmicks. Just raw, essential knowledge—distilled into an engaging, accessible volume that will deepen your understanding of Wicca, Witchcraft, and Pagan traditions.

Business Summit Collection

A powerhouse series of business books delivering expert insights on entrepreneurship, business strategy, startups, and professional development. Designed for ambitious professionals, entrepreneurs, and aspiring business owners, this collection distills wisdom from top business minds and real-world success stories. Each volume in the series offers actionable guidance, proven strategies, and inspiring case studies – from launching innovative startups to mastering leadership and growth tactics. Whether you're looking to ignite a new venture or elevate your current business, the Business Summit Collection provides the knowledge and tools to thrive in the 21st-century business landscape. Join thousands of readers in discovering cutting-edge ideas and practical advice to drive your success.

101 Business Ideas – High Potential Businesses for the 21st Century

Looking to launch a successful business in today's world? 101 Business Ideas – High Potential Businesses for the 21st Century is your ultimate guide

to turning inspiration into enterprise. This comprehensive book unveils 101 innovative business ventures across various industries.

MARKETING Summarized

Master the Art of Branding, Digital Strategies, and Customer Engagement in the Modern Era

Step into the dynamic world of marketing like never before! This isn't just another textbook—it's

your ultimate guide to mastering the strategies, tools, and innovations that drive today's most successful brands. Unlock your potential.

ENTREPRENEURSHIP Summarized

The Complete Guide to Starting, Growing, and Scaling a Successful Business

This is not just another book about entrepreneurship—it's your blueprint for building

something extraordinary, for breaking free from the ordinary, and for redefining what's possible. Are you ready to take the leap?

PRODUCT DEVELOPMENT Summarized

A Comprehensive Guide to Creating, Launching, and Managing Market-Winning Products

Every groundbreaking product starts with a spark—but only those who master the journey from idea to market truly succeed. Are you ready to join their ranks? [...] This book will give you the edge you need to succeed in a fast-moving, competitive world. Don't just develop products—shape the future.

SUPPLY CHAIN Summarized

A Comprehensive Guide to Strategies, Analytics, and Innovations for Efficient, Resilient, and Sustainable Supply Chains

In a world where supply chains power every industry—from the gadgets in your hand to the food on your table—mastering the art and science behind them has never been more critical. Are you ready to transform challenges into opportunities and lead in the age of interconnected global commerce?

PRODUCTION Summarized

A Comprehensive Guide to Efficient Manufacturing, Lean Systems, and Sustainable Production for Business Success

A Comprehensive Guide to Efficient Manufacturing, Lean Systems, and Sustainable Production for Business Success [...] your blueprint for success. Your journey to production mastery begins here. Let's build something extraordinary.

OPERATION MANAGEMENT Summarized

Master the Fundamentals of Operations, Supply Chains, and Process Optimization for Business Success

Unlock the secrets to operational excellence and take your business to new heights! In today's fast-paced, hyper-competitive world, mastering Operation Management isn't just a skill—it's a necessity. Dive in today and lead your business to operational success!

MANAGEMENT Summarized

A Comprehensive Guide to Mastering Leadership, Strategy, and Organizational Success

Unlock the Secrets to Mastering Leadership, Strategy, and Organizational Success. If you're ready to step into your full potential, lead with confidence,

and create lasting impact, this is the book for you. Transform your career. Transform your world.

PROJECT MANAGEMENT Summarized

The Ultimate Guide to Mastering Agile, Risk, and Resource Strategies for Successful Projects

In the fast-paced world of business and innovation, project management is the superpower that transforms ideas into reality.

Don't just manage projects—own them. Step into the driver's seat of your career, empowered with strategies that turn challenges into opportunities.

COMPETITION Summarized

Master the Fundamentals, Strategies, and Future Trends to Dominate Competitive Markets

In a world where every decision can mean the difference between triumph and failure, competition reigns supreme. From boardrooms to battlefields,

from bustling markets to global megacorporations, competition drives progress, fuels innovation, and shapes the future of industries and societies.

HUMAN RESOURCES Summarized

A Comprehensive Guide to HR Strategies, Practices, and Trends for Success in the Modern Workplace

Unlock the secrets to mastering the art and science of managing people in today's dynamic business world. Perfect for professionals and

newcomers alike, this is the one book your career — and your organization — cannot afford to miss. The future of HR is here. Are you ready to lead it?

Philosophy Summit Collection

Are you ready to explore the essence of wisdom and discover how great thinkers have shaped our world across centuries?

The Philosophy Summit Collection is your passport to a universe of philosophical ideas, bridging ancient and modern perspectives in a compelling, accessible way. Whether you're new to philosophy or seeking fresh insights, each volume in this groundbreaking series unpacks history's most influential schools of thought—revealing just how powerful these concepts can be for your everyday life.

Embark on your journey today, starting with our flagship title or any of the specialized volumes that catch your eye. It's time to climb the summit of thought and discover the heights of insight!

101 Philosophy Ideas - Timeless Wisdom to Empower Your Thinking and Your Life

Step into a fascinating introduction to philosophy that unites ancient wisdom with modern thought, giving you the ultimate roadmap to understand the history of philosophy and harness it for personal transformation. 101 Philosophy Ideas is your philosophy guide to the theories, thinkers, and debates that have shaped Western and Eastern philosophy alike—from Aristotle and Confucius to Nietzsche and beyond.

STOICISM Summarized

Ancient Wisdom for Modern Resilience: Mastering Mindset, Discipline, and Virtue for a Fulfilled Life

What if the secret to a powerful, unshakable mind was discovered over two thousand years ago? What if the path to true freedom, resilience, and success didn't lie in chasing wealth or external validation, but in mastering your own thoughts and actions? Are you ready to become Stoic?

EASTERN PHILOSOPHY Summarized

Timeless Wisdom from Hinduism, Buddhism, Daoism, and Confucianism for Mindfulness, Ethics, and Enlightenment

Transform Your Mind, Your Life, and Your Understanding of Reality! Are you ready to embark on a journey of transformation and insight? The path begins here.

EXISTENTIALISM Summarized

A Concise Guide to Freedom, Meaning, and the Absurd in Philosophy, Life, and Society

What does it mean to truly exist? Are we free, or are we trapped by forces beyond our control? If life has no inherent meaning, how do we create our own?

This is more than philosophy—it's a call to action. Will you choose to live authentically? The abyss is staring back. Are you ready to stare back at it?

CRITICAL THINKING Summarized

The Ultimate Guide for Mastering Logic, Thinking Smarter, Spoting Lies and Making Better Decisions

We live in an era of misinformation, logical fallacies, and relentless persuasion—an age where half-truths spread faster than facts, and biased

reasoning can lead entire societies astray. Critical Thinking Summarized is your weapon against deception, manipulation, and flawed reasoning.

ETHICS Summarized

Understanding Right and Wrong: A Complete Overview of Ethical Theories and Moral Reasoning

What is right? What is wrong? And why does it matter? From the dawn of civilization to the rise of artificial intelligence, humanity has wrestled with

moral dilemmas that define our existence. Are you ready to think deeply, argue boldly, and challenge everything you thought you knew about morality?

PHILOSOPHY OF MIND Summarized

Exploring Consciousness, Free Will, AI, and the Nature of Thought

What is consciousness? Can we trust our perceptions? Do we have free will, or are we just complex machines running on neural code? If you've

ever questioned reality, if you've ever wondered what makes you you—this is the book you've been waiting for.

POLITICAL PHILOSOPHY Summarized

Key Thinkers, Theories, and Debates on Power, Justice, and Freedom—From Plato to Postmodernism

What is justice? Who should rule? Can power ever be legitimate? This is no dry academic textbook. It's a bold, accessible, and razor-sharp and everything you need to master political philosophy—without the fluff, jargon, or confusion.. Understand the past. Decipher the present. Shape the future.

PHILOSOPHY OF RELIGION Summarized

A Concise Guide to Faith, Reason, God, and the Big Questions of Existence – Arguments, Critiques, and Key Debates in Religious Philosophy

What is the nature of God? Can faith and reason truly coexist? Why do some find deep meaning in religion while others reject it outright? Is there a way to settle the debate once and for all?

ANCIENT GREEK PHILOSOPHY Summarized

A Complete Guide to the Thinkers, Ideas, and Legacy of Classical Philosophy—From Socrates to Aristotle and Beyond

What does it mean to live a good life? What is truth, and how do we find it? Can reason shape society, or is chaos inevitable? These are not just questions for scholars in ivory towers—they are the foundations of how we think, act, and live today. The wisdom of the ancients awaits.

NIETZSCHE Summarized

Understanding Nietzsche: A Clear Guide to His Most Powerful and Controversial Ideas

What if everything you believed about truth, morality, and human nature was an illusion? What if God were dead, and you were left to forge your own path in a world without absolute meaning? If you are ready to think dangerously, live courageously, and go beyond good and evil, then this book is for you.

Psychology Summit Collection

Unlock the secrets of the mind and drive your personal growth to new heights with the Psychology Summit Collection – a comprehensive library of psychology wisdom. This series brings together holistic analyses of psychology, cognitive science, and human behavior with concise reference guides, giving you the ultimate toolkit for understanding the mind and applying its lessons in everyday life. Whether you're a psychology enthusiast, a business professional, a student, or on a self-improvement journey, this collection will elevate your knowledge and empower you to influence behavior and achieve lasting change.

Start your ascent with the Psychology Summit Collection today – and become the master of your mind.

101 Psychology Ideas - Understand the Mind, Influence Behavior, and Achieve Lasting Change

What if you could crack the code of the human mind and use it to improve every aspect of your life? 101 Psychology Ideas is your ultimate field guide to

understanding how minds work and applying psychology to influence behavior and spark positive change. Take the first step toward lasting change and empowerment.

FAMILY PSYCHOLOGY Summarized
The Ultimate Guide to Family Dynamics, Parenting, Relationships, and Mental Health—Insights for Stronger Bonds and Lasting Happiness

What makes a family thrive? Why do some

relationships deepen over time while others fracture under pressure? How can you foster resilience, love, and emotional intelligence in your household?

MOTHER AND CHILD PSYCHOLOGY Summarized
The Science of Maternal Bonding, Child Development, and Parenting Strategies for Lifelong Emotional and Cognitive Growth

What makes a mother's love so powerful? How

does early bonding influence a child's intelligence, resilience, and sense of self? Why do some children thrive while others struggle emotionally? Unlock the Science of Mother-Child Bonding

FATHER AND CHILD PSYCHOLOGY Summarized

The Essential Guide to Parenting, Attachment, and Child Development for Stronger Father-Child Bonds

What does it truly mean to be a father? How does a man shape the mind, heart, and future of his child? Drawing from the latest psychological research and timeless wisdom, this book delves into the essential role of fathers—from the earliest days of infancy to adulthood. Fatherhood is not just a role—it is a legacy. Start building yours today.

SOCIAL PSYCHOLOGY Summarized

The Ultimate Guide to Human Behavior, Influence, and Decision-Making – Master Social Dynamics, Persuasion, and Psychological Triggers

What if you could decode every social interaction with scientific precision? What if you could persuade, influence, and connect with people effortlessly—whether in business, relationships, or everyday life? Are you ready to unlock the psychology of influence, persuasion, and social dynamics?

COGNITION Summarized

The Ultimate Guide to Understanding the Mind: Theories, Processes, and Practical Applications of Cognitive Science

What if you could unlock the mysteries of your own mind? What if you could master the art of thinking, decision-making, learning, and creativity like never before? Unlock the secrets of cognition. Transform the way you think. Buy your copy today.

PERCEPTION Summarized

A Comprehensive Guide to Understanding Human Perception: How We See, Hear, Feel, and Interpret Reality Across Senses, Cultures, and Technologies

What if everything you see, hear, and feel isn't what it seems? Rich with insights into vision, hearing, taste, touch, memory, and more, this book doesn't just explain perception—it shows you why it matters. Uncover how perception defines your reality.

PERSONALITY Summarized

A Comprehensive Guide to Traits, Theories, and Self-Discovery for Personal Growth and Success

Unlock the Secrets of Who You Are and Who You Can Become. What truly defines you? Are you born with your personality, or does the world shape it? Can you change who you are—or are you destined to remain the same? Are you ready to take control of your personality—and your destiny? Start your journey today.

BEHAVIOURAL PSYCHOLOGY Summarized

The Ultimate Guide to Understanding Human Behavior, Conditioning, and Behavior Modification Techniques

Unlock the Secrets of Human Behavior and Take Control of Your Life! Why do people act the way they do? How can habits be broken, behaviors reshaped, and decisions influenced? Prepare to see the world differently. And more importantly—learn how to change it.

DEVELOPMENTAL PSYCHOLOGY Summarized

Essential Guide to Human Growth, Behavior, and Lifespan Development - Key Theories, Research, and Practical Insights

Unlock the Secrets of Human Development – From Birth to Beyond! Why do we think, feel, and grow the way we do? How do childhood experiences shape our future? What drives personality, intelligence, and emotions across the lifespan? Are you ready to decode the blueprint of human development? Start your journey today!

Printed in Great Britain
by Amazon

60883990R00107